Help a Child Learn to Read

Judy Blankenship
Cheatham, Ph.D.

Produced by the Region III Comprehensive Center,
The George Washington University Center for Equity and
Excellence in Education in collaboration with
Literacy Volunteers of America, Inc.

This printing made possible by a grant from the
Independent Telecommunications Pioneer Association.

About the Region III Comprehensive Center

The Region III Comprehensive Center (R3CC) serves Delaware, the District of Columbia, Maryland, New Jersey, Ohio, and Pennsylvania. As one of 15 federally funded comprehensive centers created with the passage of the Improving America's Schools Act in 1994, the Center provides high-quality technical assistance to states, districts and schools. R3CC supports school improvement initiatives that focus on improving teaching and learning and ensuring equitable opportunities for all students to achieve high academic standards. The Center's legislative mandate requires that special priority is given to supporting schoolwide programs and school districts with the highest concentrations of children in poverty. The R3CC is a project of the Center for Equity and Excellence in Education at the George Washington University in partnership with RMC Research Corporation (Portsmouth, NH), Research for Better Schools (Philadelphia, PA), and ESCORT (Oneonta, NY).

The Center for Equity and Excellence in Education (CEEE) was established to promote systemwide educational reform aimed at improving the achievement of all students. In addition to housing the Region III Comprehensive Center, CEEE currently is conducting Trading Partners, a national study examining promising practices among schools that improve the continuity of education for migrant children. The Center also develops resources for and provides technical assistance to educators serving English Language Learners, including Promoting Excellence, a series of publications designed to create school climates that ensure academic success for limited English proficient students.

The R3CC is located at 1730 N. Lynn St., Suite 401, Arlington, VA 22209.

About Literacy Volunteers of America, Inc.

Literacy Volunteers of America, Inc. (LVA) is a national, nonprofit, educational organization founded in Syracuse, New York, by Ruth Colvin in 1962. LVA provides materials and services to assist in the development of volunteer tutorial programs in Basic Literacy (BL) and English for Speakers of Other Languages (ESOL) for adults and teens throughout the United States and Canada. Professional and volunteer staff members are trained to manage local programs. Tutors assist adults and teens to read, write, understand, and speak English. LVA has an active network of state organizations and midlevel systems to support its almost 400 affiliated programs. Extending beyond its affiliates, LVA's training materials and related services are used by organizations and programs in libraries, churches, correctional facilities, adult basic education and public school classes, colleges, and universities. Since its founding, LVA has stressed learner-centered instruction and the use of real-world materials to promote literacy and English language acquisition.

Little Bear ©1957 by Else Holmeland Minarik. Used by permission of Harper Collins Publishers.

Literacy Volunteers of America, Inc.
635 James St., Syracuse, NY 13203
Phone: 1-800-582-8812 • Fax: 315-472-0002

ISBN 0-930713-97-4
LVA Order #49005

About the Author

Judy Blankenship Cheatham, Ph.D., LVA Writing Consultant

Judy Cheatham is the Campbell Professor of Writing and Professor of English at Greensboro College, North Carolina. The author of *Small Group Tutoring: A Collaborative Approach for Literacy Instruction,* and coauthor of *TUTOR 7* and *Whole Language for Adults,* she has been active in family and workplace literacy since 1986. She has conducted adult and family literacy projects underwritten by grants from the National Endowment for the Humanities, the U.S. Department of Education, the Kentucky Humanities Council, and the Kentucky Literacy Commission. In her literary work, Dr. Cheatham has trained thousands of tutors across the country.

At Greensboro College, Dr. Cheatham teaches linguistics, Modern English, composition, American and women's literature, and three pedagogy courses (The Pedagogy of Middle Grades Language Arts, the Pedagogy of Teaching English to Speakers of Other Languages, and the Pedagogy of English, Grades 9-12); she also is involved with training, planning, and supervising in the College's extensive field experience and tutoring programs offered through the Teacher Education Program. She sits on the Lindley Elementary School PTA board, the Grimsley High School advisory committee, the LVA local affiliate Reading Connections board, and the O. Henry Festival board, serving in 1998 as chair.

A teacher since 1973, Dr. Cheatham lives in Greensboro with her husband, George, and two children, Dayton and Sarah Hampton.

Help a Child Learn to Read was produced under Cooperative Agreement No. S283A50040 from the U.S. Department of Education to the Center for Equity and Excellence in Education at The George Washington University. The contents of this publication do not necessarily reflect the views or policies of the U.S. Department of Education or any agency of the U.S. Government.

This work includes material from *TUTOR, 7th edition,* copyright 1993 by Literacy Volunteers of America, Inc.

PROJECT DIRECTOR: C. MILLAR BRACE
CONTENT EDITOR: MARCIA REINHOLTZ
DESIGN: DEBORAH A. DiROMA, CREATIVE FX

Acknowledgments

I am delighted to have the task of writing *Help a Child Learn to Read*. Having been teaching since 1973 and working with Literacy Volunteers of America since 1986, I have long thought there should be a natural marriage between the classroom and carefully trained tutors, a win-win situation for all involved. As Ruth Colvin, Lester Laminack, and I wrote *Tutor 7*, we constantly noted how badly this type of manual was needed for tutors of children, a manual that could combine LVA's vast knowledge about what works in tutoring with current theory and best practice in reading, yet presented in language easily understood by the lay person.

In addition to my work in adult literacy, I have had the opportunity since 1990 to train hundreds of adult and college student volunteers to work in the schools. I have been able to see for myself what works and what doesn't. So when approached by LVA and George Washington University's Center for Excellence and Equity in Education to write this manual, I immediately agreed.

I am indebted to my friends and colleagues across the country who have provided encourgement and guidance in the development of this book: principal Kathryn Lofquist, Lindley Elementary School, Greensboro, NC; retired principals Dr. Nancy Routh, Greensboro, NC, and Dorothy Butler, Nashville, TN; special educator and tutor coordinator Clare Eastes, Casper College, Casper, WY; literacy professionals George Demetrion, Syracuse, NY, Mary Hausen, Salt Lake City, UT, and Phyllis Anderson, Hilton Head, SC; U.S. Department of Education staff Mary Jean LeTendre, Director of Compensatory Education Programs, Patricia McKee, Carol Hampton Rasco, Senior Advisor to the Secretary and Director, America Reads Challenge, Mary LeGwin, and Elizabeth Powers; Dr. Charlene Rivera and Kristina Anstrom, The George Washington University Center for Excellence and Equity in Education; parent Melanie Decker, Greensboro, NC; tutoring coordinator Kathy Phillips, Meadowview After School Tutoring Program, Mt. Airy, NC schools; teacher assistant/small group tutor Emily Kitchen, Lindley Elementary school. As always, it has been a pleasure to work with Millar Brace, LVA Director of Publishing.

I especially thank six people: First, my colleague Marcia Reinholtz, Ed.D. When Millar Brace asked me about a content editor, I told him that we needed someone with early childhood, elementary education, and special education licensures as well as a counseling background. He asked how many folks we'd have to hire to satisfy all those requirements. As I was thinking about individuals, Dr. Reinholtz' name came immediately to mind. As content editor, she has been a thorough reader, an excellent critic, and a good teacher. She is knowledgeable, efficient, and gentle.

Second, my husband, George Cheatham, Ph.D. Because he is a good husband and father, I have opportunities to write. He is also an exceptional writer and editor, and has graciously donated his time and talents to read this text.

Third, Greensboro College Humanities secretary Melanie Decker, a computer whiz and the fastest typist in town. She has sat with me after hours and during breaks, checking page by page. Melanie, the mother of five-year-old Mikey, has also "field tested" the manual at home.

Fourth, my mother, June Wheeler Blankenship. A 1987 Metro Nashville Teacher of the Year, she has taught little children to read for over 50 years. She volunteered to share her knowledge of what to do with the earliest beginner. The results of her labors are a very child-centered text, Chapter Five, and tutor-and-child friendly appendices.

Finally, I thank my own two children, Dayton and Sarah Hampton, both strong readers and writers. I watched Dayton "read" at five months when "reading" meant trying to eat the pictures of baby animals in his books. With him, I learned not to say "sound it out" as we read *The Little Blue Brontosaurus* before bed. At two, Sarah Hampton "wrote" me love notes. She'd decorate a page with letters or wavy lines, then say, "Dear Mommy, I love you best. You are the best mommy in the world. Love, your baby Sarah Hampton Cheatham."

Through the generous endowment of Ruth and Jack Campbell to Greensboro College, I have time and energy to devote to humanitarian pursuits like this. I also owe much to my colleagues and good friends Ruth Colvin, founder of Literacy Volunteers of America, and Dr. Lester Laminack, and I gratefully acknowledge their work.

To children everywhere and to those who strive to help them, I dedicate this book.

J.B.C.

Table of Contents

Table of Contents

Introduction 1

Chapter 1
  When "Read to Me" becomes
  "Read with Me" 3

Chapter 2
  Common Questions 9

Chapter 3
  Reading 35

Chapter 4
  Techniques Used in Collaborative Tutoring 49

Chapter 5
  "Let's Start at the Very Beginning" 87

Appendices 103

Literacy Volunteers of America, Inc.

Introduction

Introduction

Reading has long been the foundation of learning, self-sufficiency, and productive employment. As we move into the 21st century, all children will need to achieve levels of literacy higher than ever before in order to participate in America's high-skill workplaces. To address this need, President Clinton has summoned every American to join his America Reads Challenge to help more children read well and independently by the end of third grade.

The Region III Comprehensive Center (R3CC) at The George Washington University's Center for Equity and Excellence in Education is responding to the President's call. Through its mission to improve teaching and learning so that all children can achieve high standards, the Center has initiated a collaborative effort with Literacy Volunteers of America to develop *Help a Child Learn to Read: A Manual for Tutoring in Schools.* This manual is intended for those who are willing to spend time, thought, and effort to help young children learn to read. The R3CC has committed its energy and resources to developing and sharing research-based practices in literacy education to assist those involved with this critical aspect of a child's development.

Help a Child Learn to Read is yet another example of R3CC's commitment to this goal. Individuals with expertise in literacy education from the R3CC and Literacy Volunteers of America have been involved in the planning and writing of the manual. Together, we invite you to use it as a guide, not a prescription, in helping children learn to read.

Charlene Rivera, Ed.D.
Executive Director and Senior Research Scientist,
Center for Equity and Excellence in Education,
The George Washington University

Chapter One

Chapter One

When "Read to Me" Becomes "Read with Me"

When I was a little girl, one of four children, I loved it when I was sick and able to stay home from school. That meant I had my mother all to myself. She made me chicken soup, I drank CocaCola, and we read. As I snuggled under the covers, she lay beside me and read from an old book, one with which my grandmother had begun her teaching in the mountains of Ashe County, North Carolina. She opened my mind to wonderful things – Ichabod Crane and Sleepy Hollow; Rip Van Winkle; The Gingham Dog and the Calico Cat; Barefoot Boy with cheeks of tan; Wynken, Blynken and Nod; Hiawatha and the shores of Gitchee Goomee. "What is so rare as a day in June?" I heard first at age seven.

What are your early memories of reading? For most of us, there was someone —mother, father, grandparent, teacher, older sister or brother—into whose lap we could climb or beside whom we could snuggle as we requested, "Read to me." To many, one of life's precious moments occurs the first time a child then says to us, "Read to me."

There comes the time, though, when "read to me" changes to "read with me." Every child has to learn for herself or himself what we, thankfully, have learned: how to "call" words; how to take print, decode it, and understand it; how to make sense out of written language; in other words, how to read.

Even if you never had someone read with you or to you as a child, now you want to provide that opportunity for a child in your life—your own, a friend's or relative's, or perhaps a perfect stranger's child whom you are about to meet through tutoring at home, at school, at church, in the library, or at the community center.

You want to help a child learn to "read with" you. You want to tutor!

However excited you may feel, you may also be nervous, wondering if you can actually learn how to teach reading to someone else. In fact, you may have looked at some reading guides and felt that you would need a graduate degree in reading to understand them. This book is written for you, for all of you who are willing to expend your efforts to help children become independent readers and writers. Its purpose is to present professionally accepted approaches and techniques with step-by-step instructions for tutoring on a one-to-one basis, but to do so in the language of the lay person, to avoid all attempts at overly technical discussions.

In fact, the text is based on answers to twenty questions often asked by parents and tutors. As you read, you will find answers to the following:

1. Does tutoring make a difference?

2. What is reading?

3. How is reading different from the other language components of listening, speaking, and writing?

4. How does the tutor know if the child comprehends what that child is reading?

5. What does research tell us about the place of phonics in reading instruction?

6. What should the tutor do when a child stumbles over or misreads a word?

7. When and how does a tutor introduce writing?

8. How does the tutor evaluate student performance?

9. Based on the evaluation, how can the tutor then plan effective tutoring to address the child's individual needs?

10. How often should a person tutor?

11. How long should a tutor commit to tutoring?

12. Where should the tutor and student meet?

13. How does the tutor know what material to cover?

14. How do the tutor and child choose an appropriate book to read?

15. How can a tutor create activities for reading from almost any reading material, including the content areas of science, social studies and mathematics?

16. What is meant by age-appropriateness and how does it relate to tutoring?

17. How does the tutor begin when the child does not even know the ABCs?

18. How does the tutor work with a child who is learning English?

19. How does the tutor document the material covered?

20. What support should the tutor seek?

Some of these questions are explicitly answered in Chapter Two, some implicitly throughout.

Help a Child Learn to Read contains

- a theoretical and attitudinal base from which to tutor

- discussions of needed skills and approaches for tutoring

- examples and demonstrations to illustrate theories, concepts, techniques, and activities.

Interwoven throughout the text are these underlying themes, adopted by Literacy Volunteers of America, that you will be putting into practice as you tutor:

1. A respect for each student as an individual

2. A view of the tutor and the student as both learners and teachers

3. A sensitivity to the importance of an immediate or relevant context

4. A view of tutoring and learning as collaborative activities

5. An integration of all four language components.

> All human beings are at one time or another both students and teachers. When it is your turn to teach, you must respect your student as a human being fully worthy and deserving of human dignity, no matter your or the student's age. As a tutor, you must respect the student's rights to:

- hold views different from yours

- have language patterns that do not match yours or the dominant culture's

- have goals or interests different from the ones you might choose for that student.

In essence, you want to treat the student as you yourself like to be treated. Read this book, attend tutor trainings and workshops, practice the techniques and activities. Use the book as a springboard to deepen your own understanding, to explore your assumptions, and to build your knowledge of reading and tutoring. Have your own conversation with the text: write in the margins, highlight important ideas, make note of those things you find helpful and those things you want to reread later. Remember, though, to apply all situations to yourself. How would you like to be treated in these various cases? That should keep you on target as you tutor.

The George Washington University Center for Equity and Excellence in Education and Literacy Volunteers of America invite you to join us and thousands of others across the country as together we work with people who need help in reading and writing. As you help others, as you touch individual lives, you too will be touched. Your life will never be the same.

And when the child says, "Read with me," you will be ready.

Literacy Volunteers of America, Inc.

Chapter Two

DOES TUTORING MAKE A DIFFERENCE?

- One-to-One Addresses Needs of the Child
- Tutoring Provides Support or "Scaffold" for Learning
- Tutoring Provides Additional Opportunities for the Child to Learn and Practice Skills and Concepts from the Classroom
- Effective Tutoring Programs Coordinate and Support the Tutor's Efforts

HOW OFTEN SHOULD I TUTOR?

HOW MANY WEEKS SHOULD I TUTOR?

WHERE SHOULD MY STUDENT AND I MEET?

HOW DO I CHOOSE A BOOK?

- Discover What the Child Likes
- Find Books That Are Reader-Friendly
- Identify Predictable Books
- Make Friends with the Children's Librarians at Your Local Library

WHAT IS MEANT BY AGE-APPROPRIATE?

WHAT DO I DO IF THE CHILD I AM TUTORING DOES NOT SPEAK ENGLISH?

HOW DO I KNOW WHERE TO START WITH MY STUDENT?

- Informal Assessment

HOW DO I PLAN LESSONS AND KEEP RECORDS?

The Portfolio

The Elements of a Lesson

- Greeting
- Reading
- Comprehension Check
- Skills
- Writing
- Reading for Pleasure

SUMMARY

Chapter Two
Common Questions

This chapter presents some of the most common questions tutors ask before they begin or during their tutoring. Read the chapter and then, as you read through the rest of the book, you may want to return here from time to time as the need arises. This chapter has a heavy research basis; if you want to explore some of the ideas here, the Works Cited section in the Appendices should provide you with a starting point. The question not addressed here is how to deal with a child with learning differences. Chapters Three and Four infuse discussion of exceptionalities throughout.

Does Tutoring Make a Difference?

Before you embark upon this endeavor, it is only natural to ask yourself if tutoring a child is actually going to make a difference in what that child learns. To answer that question, we can go to the research, to the many studies done over the past two decades. These studies tell us that, yes, an effective tutoring program has a significant, positive impact on children's learning for several reasons. (See Bloom; Clay & Cazden; Cohen, Kulik, & Kulik; Devin-Sheehan, Feldman, & Allen; Greenwood, Delquardi, & Hall; Hiebert; Jenkins, & Jenkins; Juel; McLeary; Topping; Wasik & Slavin; Wood, Bruner, & Ross.)

First, one-to-one tutoring addresses the needs of the child.

The one-to-one relationship between the child and the tutor allows the tutor to concentrate on the specific learning needs of the child. In an effective tutoring program, the tutor can provide his or her undivided attention to one child, addressing the very specific needs of that one child in a way that the classroom teacher—unless the teacher has a very small class size—is physically not able to do. Though the teacher is a trained professional, sometimes situations fall outside his or her control. For example, consider the class of 29 children of differing needs and backgrounds, with differing abilities. One teacher would have trouble preparing 29 specialized lessons and delivering them 29 times during the day. Physically, this tests the limits of any human being. However, in an effective tutoring program–one in which the tutor, the teacher, the child, and often the parent are in communication—the tutor can provide that one-to-one instruction individualized to the particular strengths and needs of the child.

We know, for example, that among the several skills and attitudes that affect success in reading are these:

- knowing the alphabet

- knowing sounds and their symbols

- understanding the concept of "print" (e.g., knowing that letters make up words, words make up sentences, words and sentences express thoughts, etc.)

- having a wide vocabulary to describe the world around us

- knowing spelling patterns

- reading easily and correctly an increasing number of words

- reading reflectively.

In our hypothetical class of 29 students, suppose one child needs help desperately with sound-symbol relationships. The teacher has focused on certain sounds, but this child has not been able to grasp what the teacher has presented to the class. Another child understands the sound-symbol correspondence but does not understand that a word consists of a group of letters put together, with a first and last letter. Yet a third child has a very limited speaking vocabulary. Still a fourth, fifth, and sixth child speak languages other than English at home. Tutors in one-to-one tutoring situations can spend time intervening in the particular areas of need for each of these particular six children. Clearly, this type of child-centered intervention is effective and efficient. The tutor, in a one-to-one situation, is able to provide individual instruction targeted at the individual child's areas of need.

Second, tutoring provides a support or "scaffold" for learning.

Effective one-to-one tutoring relationships often resemble the "parent-child dyad" that helps children learn. Across the globe, Dr. Jerome Bruner and others have observed parents helping children learn. What so often occurs in these situations is that the parents provide a kind of support, even a kind of instructional or linguistic "scaffold," that supports children as they learn. J. Wertsch, for example, describes the way preschoolers learn to work puzzles through interaction with their mothers, the puzzle, and the puzzle pieces. At the first level, the mother redefines for the child what needs to be done to put the puzzle together. At the second level, the child watches the mother as she does the task, explaining again and in other ways what she is doing. At the third level, the child and the mother share the task; together, they work the puzzle. The mother and child talk out the task as they perform it. At the fourth level, the child is able to perform the task alone. In this type of scaffolded learning situation, the task is broken into pieces by the mother. Her "scaffold" allows the child plenty of explanations about the task and plenty of opportunities to try it with her before the child actually tries to put the puzzle back together alone. The mother's expectation is that the child will be successful, no matter how many times the parent and child repeat the process, no matter how many times she and her child talk through the process.

Dr. Bruner describes for us the ways in which infants acquire language through a process very similar to the one above. Mothers, fathers, or primary caregivers, Dr. Bruner says, provide linguistic scaffolding for their babies, removing the scaffolds when they are no longer necessary or replacing them with other, more sophisticated scaffolds. For example, the adult (mother or whoever) at first provides the entire conversation as the baby merely grunts, cries, or gurgles. "Baby want a bottle?" she asks over and over, and then she answers her own question, "Yes, baby want a bottle." Later, learning to talk, the baby points or grabs at something he wants while articulating what vaguely resembles the name of the object ("cookie," for example). The mother then has to figure out the object of the baby's desire, so she supplies the appropriate scaffold: "Cookie?" she guesses,

"Do you want a cookie?" The baby's verbal response varies: "Mine," he may say; "Me want" or "Me want cookie" are also possibilities—as is a loud, "No!" By age two or so, the typically developing toddler can usually ask, "Me have cookie, mommy?" He may even demand, "I want cookie." The mother can "raise" the linguistic scaffold a level at this point because the toddler is now talking in sentences. The toddler no longer needs the adult to supply the entire conversation. Now the mother can modify her input. If the toddler demands, the mother can ask, "What's the magic word?" or "How do we ask nicely?" She is seeking to hear the word "Please." Interestingly, the parent uses constant repetitions and constant praise, always expecting that the baby will learn to talk.

By the same token, the tutor can develop a similar supportive relationship with a child. The tutor can talk the child through an activity concerning a concept or skill, then repeat the activity time and again until the child develops or acquires the skill or concept and then is able to perform it with some degree of fluency. Because the situation is one-to-one, with no demands to "hurry up and get things done," the pressure sometimes present in the classroom is removed. And the tutor, like the parent or caregiver, should have the expectation of success, the expectation that every child will learn to read, no matter how many hours are spent working with that child.

Tutoring provides additional opportunities for a child to learn and practice the skills and concepts being introduced in the regular classroom.

In the most effective programs, the tutor supports the work in the classroom, addressing the grade-appropriate expectations and the curriculum currently being covered in the child's class. To understand how those tutoring programs tied to the expectations of a child's classroom make a greater impact than those not related, think back to our hypothetical class of 29. Suppose in that class is a little boy who has a set of typical classroom materials he must master. Let's say that this particular week the teacher is concentrating on short *a* words: *cat, rat, sat, can, ran, fan, as, has,* for example. He has written work daily, and he has a book he is supposed to be reading for pleasure every evening because he needs additional help to meet the teacher's expectations, his parents have enrolled him in a tutoring program. The child and his father take the homework and the reading book to the tutoring sessions. The tutor is then able to plan tutoring sessions according to what the child needs for success in the classroom.

Think of the complications, however, if the tutoring program were not connected to the child's classroom expectations. What if for that week the tutor had chosen color words for the lesson? The student and tutor would spend time on red, blue, yellow, white, black. And instead of working on the book the child has been assigned to read, what if the tutor had chosen yet another book to work on at the tutoring session? So instead of having to master one set of words, the child would then have two sets; and instead of having to read and comprehend one book, the child would then have two. Such a situation would fragment learning and confuse the child. Instead of reinforcing skills and concepts and instead of developing fluency, such a tutoring session would actually create another whole set of demands and expectations. When tutoring is not coordinated with classroom expectations, the child—who by the very fact that he needs tutoring is academically fragile—has two different sets of expectations and assignments. This second set of demands divides his attention as it fragments and complicates his concentration. It is much more efficient and effective to work on material that helps the child to participate more fully in the classroom rather than to feel marginalized because he does not "know" what the other children know or because he can not "do" what they do.

If at all possible, the program coordinator, the school principal, or some school appointed individual should supply you with a list of expectations, skills, and competencies for the grade level of the child you are tutoring. These vary from system to system, state to state. If this information is not available, certainly use as a guide the kindergarten-third grade curriculum listed in Appendix A. There you will find grade-level expectations and a short bibliography of books at the appropriate levels.

As you volunteer to tutor, you might want to consider tutoring in a program that cooperates and coordinates with the school district or local school. Such a program is usually the most effective, efficient way for the teacher, too. Instead of five tutors asking a teacher about age-appropriate or grade-appropriate materials and expectations, the program coordinator can have that information available for every tutor. In a coordinated program, everybody wins—the teacher, the tutor, the parent, and most importantly the child.

Effective tutoring programs coordinate and support tutors' efforts.

A real strength of effective tutoring programs across the country is on-going support for tutors. Though we tend to think chiefly of the needs of the students, tutors need support, too. Programs with the philosophy that tutoring merely matches children with tutors and all is well often have a high attrition, or dropout, rate for tutors! Tutors can grow frustrated if there is no one to whom they can turn for answers to questions and for continuing training. What material to teach, where to look for books, how to choose appropriate reading material, where to go to tutor, how to deal with conflict or uneven learning—these are only a few of the multitude of questions that arise during tutoring, no matter how well-trained a tutor may be to begin with.

This is the management piece of the pie. Over the past 15 years or so, good management practices have been shown to make a significant difference in the effectiveness of volunteer programs. Effective programs address coordination and tutor support in different ways. Some use in-school coordinators, paid or volunteer. Some work with local school districts or with parent-teacher organizations. Still others coordinate tutoring programs through community or religious organizations. In choosing a program in which to tutor or in helping design one in your area, keep in mind that a coordinator will make the program run more efficiently and effectively.

How Often Should I Tutor?

Tutoring programs both in the United States and elsewhere seem to come in all shapes and sizes. That is, some programs use tutors on a daily basis; others, two or three times a week; still others, only once a week. Some programs meet in the summer or on weekends. The research seems to say—and so does common sense, really—that the more often the tutor is able to work with a child in reading, the more gains that child makes. Those programs that use tutors three times a week show significantly better results than those that use tutors twice a week. It seems that tutoring only once a week is not as helpful for the child. This would make sense, especially in light of what we know about the need for repetition in developing reading fluency. Best practices as they involve any kind of language learning indicate that learners benefit from sustained, systematic, multiple opportunities for practice.

For little children, length of tutoring time is also an issue, especially as we think about attention spans. Twice a week for 1.5 to 2.0 hours is the typical time spent tutoring adults. With children, though, especially those in kindergarten through second grade, 15-30 minutes seems to be a commonly used amount of time. One successful program in England uses parent tutors who work with their elementary school aged children ten minutes a day, five days each week. This program has proven to be very beneficial. Researchers—and parents—credit the consistent practice brought on by the daily work as well as the manageable period of time (almost everybody can spare ten minutes).

Practically speaking, as a tutor who is going to go somewhere else to tutor (to the school or to a community agency or library), you may not be able to tutor every day. By the same token, your tutee may not be able to attend a daily tutoring session. Two times a week might be a workable compromise. What is probably not a good idea is trying to meet once a week, with one student, for 90 minutes. That may produce more frustration on your part as well as on the child's than any gains would offset. Instead, if you would like to commit to 90 minutes of tutoring, you might tutor two or three different children, one after the other, 30 to 45 minutes each.

How Many Weeks Should I Tutor?

Ideally, you should stay with the student you are tutoring for 12 to 16 weeks. In most school settings, this amounts to a semester and falls nicely into the end of a traditional grading period. If you are at a point in your life in which you can not commit for at least this length of time, then you might want to consider waiting to tutor until you have more time. Know, also, that some programs may ask you to commit for a year.

It is really not fair for a learner—no matter what age—to have to adjust to several tutors over the course of the year. The learner and the tutor will need to build a relationship, which takes time and energy. As the tutor, you will need to learn the child's likes and dislikes, strengths and needs; you will need to learn the way he best learns; you will need to learn when he can not do and when he will not do. This process takes time and requires that you and the child trust each other.

You may find that the child will be slow to open up to you. Sometimes adult new readers will not look up, will not raise their heads, until after a few lessons; you may see similar behaviors with a child. The relationship between learner and tutor is so special that you have to be willing to nurture and cultivate it. If you view your role casually and perhaps stop tutoring after a couple of weeks, the learner often takes your disappearance as a sure sign that something is wrong with him, that he is too "slow" or not "okay." Studies show that a child is greatly affected by how he thinks "teachers" feel about him. Of course, there are times when the unexpected happens and you must suspend your tutoring; however, if you know ahead of time that you will have a difficult time committing, wait until your time is more your own.

At the end of the 12 to 16 week tutoring period, you and the student can reassess your status. Would you like to continue in your tutoring program? What have you accomplished? What goals would you like to set for the next period? This is a nice time to look at student work in the portfolio and talk about the positive effects of your relationship. Then, if you have a scheduling conflict, you can explain that you will not be able to work with the student for the next session. Of course, you can still come by and see him from time to time (lunch buddies are always nice!); you can also send him cards or exchange letters. At any rate, an agreed upon "end" to a tutoring period provides a clean break if one is needed as well as a point of reassessment if the relationship is to continue.

In rare situations, circumstances may arise that cause you to discontinue your efforts or to change students. If you ever feel threatened at all by the learner or by the learner's family or friends, immediately speak with the program coordinator or school principal. Sometimes a student might be delinquent in attending lessons. After a second or third time, you need to say very frankly, "Well, you have missed your lesson three times. I wonder if you've got so many other things you're concerned about right now that learning to read and write better is not at the top of your list. Perhaps later on you'll be ready for more lessons." If the child has to be brought to an after-school site for tutoring, the child may have no control over whether she shows up or not. In this case, you will need to talk to the parent or caregiver. Again, be honest; you are volunteering your time and you want to see someone profit from it. You might say, "Mary has missed the last three sessions. Are you having trouble getting here? Are there ways that the program could help with transportation? I am a volunteer and look forward to my sessions with Mary, but I would appreciate it if you would tell me if this semester or perhaps these next few weeks are not a good time for you."

Be sensitive as you deal with this situation. Before you take any action, discuss it with the program coordinator or teacher. Ask about situations at home that might prevent the parent from working with you. You do not want to pry, and the coordinator or teacher will certainly respect the confidentiality of the family. However, it may be that the parent does not speak or read English and does not understand the tutoring situation or his role in it. It may be that the parent does not read or write and therefore has not read or responded to material sent home. It also may be an issue of child care and/or transportation.

If you find that the parent needs information through another medium, work with the program coordinator or school personnel to make that information available. It may require a home visit, a translator, a phone call, or some combination of the three.

If the parent has other little children at home and/or no means of transportation, see what aid is available. Does the program operate a van? Does the school have a special bus?

Need for childcare, lack of transportation, and written and oral language problems are often identified as barriers to self-sufficiency. As a tutor, you will want to recognize that any or all of these three situations could be preventing the child from attending tutoring sessions. Here again a program coordinator or school personnel should address these situations.

By the same token, if you agree to meet with a child at a certain time during the week, you owe it to the child and to the program to make your commitment a priority. If for some reason you can not attend a session, you need to let the appropriate person (program coordinator, the principal, teacher, parent, etc.) know as soon as possible. At the very least, your absence can confuse the child and cause a reassigning problem for the program coordinator. At the other extreme, you could be placing the child in a precarious, even dangerous, situation if you are not where you are supposed to be. If you find yourself missing two or three times, you need to reconsider your commitment.

In a child- or learner-centered program, the child's needs are central; however, a learning relationship involves two, the learner and the tutor. It is not good practice to allow sessions to become something you dread, nor is it good practice to feel that you are not being respected as an individual. You will need to be the one to speak up about it, however. Luckily, happily, these situations are rare. Most tutors tell us that tutoring is the most rewarding activity they've ever done.

Where Should My Student and I Meet?

For some tutors, this question is moot. Your program may have sites already chosen. Programs meet in libraries, churches, businesses, YMCAs and YWCAs, school buildings—you name it. If, however, you need to choose your own site, keep in mind these guidelines. The location of your tutoring sessions may have a significant influence on the frequency and duration of your sessions. Accessibility, availability of public transportation, expense, and ride-sharing possibilities are all elements to consider. Use your own judgment, but it is not usually recommended that students come to your home or that you go to theirs—there are too many distractions to make that work and a host of other problems may crop up. Certainly, follow your program's guidelines; if your program does not have guidelines, encourage the establishment of some.

Ask your program coordinator or school principal about possible places to tutor. Common sense dictates that you will probably want to be in view of others—at a table in the media center, in a glassed-in room in a library or school, in a special part of the classroom. Each program should offer you guidelines on this subject. Ask also about what to do if the child must go to the bathroom. If there is no guideline, insist that one be established.

If you are tutoring in an in-school program, make sure that you know ahead of time whether you are to get the child from her classroom or whether she is to come to the tutoring site on her own. For a community or church-based program, you may want to call the home before the first session, clarifying the time and place.

How Do I Choose a Book?

Any or all of the following three types of books may be involved in your tutoring experience: children's literature (a story book, book of poems, etc.), a content area book like science or social studies, and a workbook. If you have the opportunity, check with the classroom teacher about the book selection. It may be that the teacher would like you to choose from a set of books in the classroom or a series to be used in the classroom. The teacher may also have a reading list to guide you. The teacher may want you to work with the child on a book the class is reading. If the child is in the third grade or above, she will probably have content area books (e.g., science, social studies, and mathematics) from which she will have assignments in reading and writing.

If, however, you are left to your own devices, below are some guidelines for choosing a book for a child in preschool or early elementary. The long and short of it is that the more you remain aware of how you like to choose your own books, the better choices you can make in helping the child. For example, when you go to the library or bookstore, you don't want some sales person taking a book out of your hands because it looks too hard or because it's too long or because he doesn't like the author. Most people walk up and down rows, choosing books from the shelves for various reasons: the titles look interesting, the artwork is different, or they have read something by that author before. Then they flip through, reading the first page or so, looking at chapters or illustrations. After they have looked through several books, they choose what they want to check out or buy. The child is no different in making this selection process; let the child choose as much as possible, although you may need to do some legwork in preparation.

First, find out what the child likes. Is he interested in dinosaurs or trains or animals? Try not to stereotype. Often, for example, little girls are just as interested in the Tyranosaurus Rex as little boys. So ask, "What do you like to do?" or "Who is your favorite cartoon character?" or "What do you like to read about?" If you are not successful in eliciting answers from the child, be patient. As you get to know the student, you will become more familiar with the likes and dislikes of that student.

Second, find some books that are "reader friendly." Children in tutoring situations often have developed negative attitudes about self as well as about print. Choose some books that look inviting. For example, look at the print. Is it large enough to see clearly? Are the words hidden by illustrations? Look for white space on the page. A page that looks too densely populated with print can overwhelm a child. You will probably want to avoid books with justified margins if you are choosing a book for beginning readers. Because the left and right justified margins make straight lines, the spaces between each word and between letters in the same word can vary as letters or words are stretched out to reach the margin. A new reader often finds this inconsistency in spacing confusing, especially since she is usually just learning that letters make up words and words make up sentences. The spaces between letters and words help the reader identify word boundaries; thus, the new reader needs consistency in the spaces between letters and between words. The new reader does not need the additional stress of having to work too hard at figuring out word boundaries. In fact, don't shy away from wordless books (like the *Good Dog, Carl* series) or books with one word per page.

Third, identify predictable books. A predictable book is one that has a refrain (e.g., "I'll huff and I'll puff and I'll blow your house down") or a pattern repeated throughout ("It looked like spilt milk . . . It looked like . . ."). The easiest of these books are often nice for a child because they allow for immediate success in reading.

Fourth, make friends with the children's librarians at your local library or with the media specialist at the school. These professionals have been working at "family literacy" since there have been libraries. They are usually able to guide you to the appropriate sections of the library and often have lists of books recommended by ease of reading. (There is also a list of recommended books by grade level in Appendix A.)

After you have identified three, four, or five books, take these with you to your first tutoring session. Place them on the table and ask the student which books look interesting. Encourage him to look at them, handle them, talk about the cover and pictures, speculate about the content of these books. Then ask, "Which one of these shall we read?" If the book seems too difficult for the child to read, do not necessarily abandon it. In Chapters Three, Four, and Five you will learn to teach phonics, word patterns, and other techniques that can be adapted in some fashion to almost any book. Thus, if the book is too difficult for the child to read but the child is really interested in it, try to use it in your lesson; realize, however, that you may need to do the bulk of the actual reading, especially at first.

Of course, it may be that the child has a favorite book. Have her bring it from home or find a copy in the library. Certainly, use this book to begin. She may know the text by heart, but you will use it to work on everything from the alphabet, to sub-skills like word patterns, to critical thinking!

Remember these points as you read to the child: first, you can do the same kind of pre-reading activities with a book you read as you would with a book the child could read himself; second, there is value in reading aloud to children, especially as you will be modeling intonation, inflection, fluency, and the running dialogue with the text; third, you can work on listening comprehension (just ask the child to summarize what is going on as you read); fourth, you can use the print of almost any page to teach the skills discussed in Chapter Four (phonics, sight words, word patterns, etc.). With the new reader, his interest in the book is the most important factor in the choice of that book.

What Is Meant by Age-Appropriate?

Age-appropriate is a term applied to expectations, materials, and instruction. Cognitively and developmentally, human beings can perform different tasks at different times in their lives. Little children, for example, are concrete learners;

19

they need to see and do. Age-appropriate materials call for active learning and allow for the child to talk, listen, hear, see, and feel. Sometimes parents and educators have expectations for children that are not within reach cognitively or developmentally; Dr. David Elkind warns that children are often "hurried" into inappropriate situations where they can not succeed. When they do not succeed, they feel failure when success was not even a possibility.

Dr. Elkind's warnings apply to tutoring situations. As we deal with little children, we need to be mindful of several areas in which we might be tempted to "push" the child either too quickly or beyond his ability. For example, developmentally, not all little children can control a pencil at age five or even six; not all little children can cut with scissors; not all little children have strong oral vocabularies.

One way to address age and developmental appropriateness is to keep in mind that little children learn through many ways. Play and art reinforce cognitive activities. Little children need multiple ways of processing information. Though their little bodies have trouble sitting still for an hour "reading," reinforcing activities help them move around as well as reinforce the concept. When you go to your session, take a tutor tote filled with developmentally appropriate materials: a glue stick, crayons, construction paper, scissors, an old magazine, an old newspaper, scrap paper, flash cards, and maybe some toys or objects that deal with your lesson.

Let's say, for example, that you are working on color words. You read a story with color words, use them with phonics activities, write them, and work with them as sight words. Then, to reinforce this learning, in your tutor tote, you could have colored paper from which to cut balloons, colored crayons to write color words, colored tissue to tear up and paste on the balloons, and so on. As you tutor, you will develop a sensitivity to the child's need to vary activities. You'll learn to help the child read a while, work on skills for a while, do reinforcing kinds of activities for a while, and listen to you read. Don't worry about going slowly. Sometimes a phonics lesson consists of working on only one or two letters, not the whole alphabet!

Because of the need to keep expectations age-appropriate, Chapter Five addresses very beginning reading strategies; also the word lists in the Appendices are presented in order of difficulty. Clearly, a reason the one-to-one tutoring situation is so successful at any age is that over time the tutor becomes familiar with the developmental level of the tutee and can offer help in specific areas of need.

The Child I Am Tutoring Does not Speak English. What Do I Do?

In our multicultural society, there is a good chance that you will tutor a child learning English as a second or subsequent language. In working with an English language learner (ELL), be mindful that this child is in the process of developing his speaking and listening ability in English, in addition to his reading and writing skills. Though learning English, the English language learner has already developed a wide variety of skills and abilities in his native or home language. He has a storehouse of words, ideas, thoughts, and dreams. He may be able to read and write. Though he may not be able to explain the "rules," he has already learned to produce sounds, make plurals, change tenses, use negatives, and ask questions, though not in English. Though languages are different, linguists tell us that every language has a sound system (phonology), a way of changing words (morphology), an ever-changing vocabulary or "dictionary" (lexicon), societal influences on vocabulary choices (semantics), and a word order (syntax). The native language is a valuable resource that the learner can use to help him understand English. Thus, a child's native language is an asset, not a hindrance, in his second language literacy development.

Children learning a second language have very different social, emotional, and intellectual needs than babies learning language for the first time. And, of course, they also have more resources than babies. Despite these differences, you may find it helpful to understand a child's development in English by reflecting upon how babies learn their first language.

First, babies do a lot of listening. Researchers tell us that a baby "hears" the equivalent of a book a day from its primary caregiver. The parent or guardian talks constantly to the baby, smiling, expecting the baby to "talk" back with coos and gurgles.

Beginning English language learners also spend a great deal of time listening; however, they listen through the "filter" of their first language, using their knowledge about how language works and applying it to learning English. Sounds that are familiar to them will be processed and used more easily than those that are new to them. When working with a child at this beginning stage, provide her with many opportunities to listen to language that is meaningful to her, language she can use immediately in the classroom, in the lunchroom, on the playground, etc.

Second, babies do a lot of looking at concrete items—things around the room, in the crib, in the house, outside, in books. The adult shows the baby object after object, repeating the names of these objects time after time. Nobody says to the baby, "Okay, baby, I told you three times that the word is 'dog.' I'm not telling you again."

Beginning ELLs also need to learn the names of objects in their environment, but unlike babies, the English language learner is probably not in the process of developing the concepts associated with these objects. For example, she knows that the word "chair" can mean the chair she is sitting on or a similarly-fashioned object in another place or time. Thus, the ELL needs to learn English words, but not necessarily the concepts associated with them, unless she has not learned the concept in her native language.

As a result, children learning words a "second" time in another language learn more quickly than do babies, and more can be expected of them. The main emphasis, though, should still be on helping the child learn English words and expressions associated with the child's life needs, not from a list in the back of a book, for example. The other lesson that can be gleaned from how a mother teaches a child her first language is the patience with which the mother repeats words and phrases. Be patient if you find that an ELL may need to have words repeated before she learns them.

Third, babies make a lot of noises before those noises turn into words. These noises are often approximations or attempts at words, but not really words. The baby begins talking—just a few words—at about six months or so. The early responses are one word responses: dada, bye-bye, no, woof woof, etc. The parent or caregiver is elated by these one word responses, giving lavish praise.

A child learning English as a second or subsequent language may also begin speaking in simple words or phrases. However, some ELLs spend a longer time listening before speaking, but when they do begin to speak, they use complete and well-formed sentences. So time spent in the "listening phase" is as varied as the children themselves. Some children may rely heavily upon the native language to fill in gaps when they don't know how to express what they want to say in English. They may also rely upon words that are similar in the native language. These words, known as cognates (e.g., *padre, pere, papa*) can greatly increase a child's comprehension of English. At this stage you can help the child extend his speech by adding onto what he has offered, by providing the linguistic scaffold. For example, if the child says, "Go home," meaning that he wishes to go home, you can extend his speech by saying, "Oh, you want to go home." Guidance in the appropriate expressions and ways of arranging words in spoken English will assist in his literacy development.

Fourth, babies don't use "good grammar." They say what they hear; then they generalize, sometimes incorrectly. When the baby says *"footsies,"* everybody around says, "Oh, isn't he smart." After a while, the baby gets older and hears enough people saying *"feet"* that he figures out the plural of "foot" is "feet." No parent ever says, "No, baby, 'foot' forms its plural irregularly, through a vowel change based on its Old English origin."

This description of how mothers interact with their babies is directly applicable to English language learners, especially when they are children. Children learn language best when correctness is modeled within a natural context, not when it is directly taught. Thus, when a child says to you, "I goed to the store yesterday," you can respond by saying, "Oh, so you went to the store yesterday. What did you buy?" Such practice models correct language for the child in the context of a conversation, in response to what he has said.

Fifth, babies learn the names of items and actions important to them: cookie, baby, doll, blankie, bottle, dog, cat, ride, mommy, daddy, water, head, eyes, ears, mouth, bathroom, go, eat, go sleep, play, no nap, mine. We don't teach babies words like kettle, folder, inoculation.

ELLs also learn what is meaningful to them. However, these objects and expressions may not be the same as for babies because these children live in very different environments. When considering what words and expressions to help the ELL with, think about what the child's needs and experiences are. What language does the child need for school, the playground, the lunchroom, the surrounding community?

Sixth, the parent or caregiver is always "testing" for comprehension, not with pencil and paper but with commands and questions: "Pat the dog," "Bring me your diaper," "Look at the pretty flower," "Which one do you want?" Of course, sometimes those commands are ignored, like "Don't throw that food on the floor," but the parent usually has a good idea if the child has understood or not!

The child learning English also needs to be tested for comprehension through questions and commands. Asher's Total Physical Response approach described below is an excellent method for both teaching and assessing a child in English listening comprehension. However, the kind of language the ELL needs to hear is now different from that which a baby needs to hear. Your instructions may include, "Bring me the book," "Close the door," "Let's walk down the hall," etc. In addition, the ELL needs to be encouraged to ask questions. He will need guidance in how to do this, how to form questions appropriately, and when to ask them. A method, such as reciprocal teaching in which the teacher first models how to ask questions related to a reading and then encourages the student to ask similar kinds of questions, can assist greatly in helping the ELL to learn how and when to question.

You can apply knowledge of how a child learns English as a second language when you are tutoring. Concentrate first on survival skills, on the things that the child needs to know to function in the classroom. It may be that much of your early work will be with listening and speaking. What does the child have to be able to say? She must give her name, her address, her age; talk about her family;

and identify classroom items and places in the school building. Teach her to say these things, writing them as you say them. By all means, make a picture dictionary (explained in Chapter Five), make tapes, let her listen to computers with voice capabilities. Use language experience (explained in Chapter Four). Concentrate on nouns and verbs. Constantly test for comprehension—take walks with her, asking her to stand beside or touch the water fountain, pick up the red book, sit in the chair, turn on the light, bring you her paper. This technique, "Total Physical Response," calls for active learning and lets you know immediately whether or not the child is understanding what you are saying.

Your first goal is to help the child to feel comfortable talking in the classroom, on the playground, and in the lunchroom. The nuances of our language will be learned over time, things like irregular plurals, verb tenses, articles, etc. What the experts call "communicative competence," however, means that people can still communicate with each other without speaking or writing perfectly in a given language.

In addition to survival language, you will need to address the demands of the class content. This is especially important for children in third grade and above. Chapters Three and Four discuss using language experience and sight word techniques to teach content area material like social studies and science. For example, you may want to work with a tape recorder if you have access to one; it is a great help to the child if she can take the tape recorder home for practice at her own pace. You can teach the child to read "George Washington," but she may need much practice in order to understand or say the phrase herself. You also will need to ensure that she knows who George Washington was and why she is learning about him. In short, you will be teaching language skills (spelling, pronunciation, listening) as well as content material.

A couple of points for caution: First, many tutors want to begin with teaching the ELL to say the ABCs. If you spend your first two weeks of instruction teaching the ABCs, what can she say after that second week? Just the ABCs. So when a potential playmate asks, "What's your name?" the new English speaking child is not able to respond. Think about it. When was the last time someone asked you to recite your ABCs? Certainly teach the ABCs, but teach them later.

Second, do not fixate on pronunciation. You and the child can both become frustrated over attempts at perfect pronunciation. Linguists now tell us that near-native pronunciation comes with time and usually only if the speaker learns the second language early in life. The younger a person is when learning a second or subsequent language, the easier it is to acquire a native accent. Children learn by talking and listening, by interactions with native speakers. You can help your student feel comfortable as she talks, plays and works with others.

Third, don't advise the parents to abandon their home language and speak English at home. Because the child acquires language through interactions with others, she needs to develop fully in her home language, taught to her by the native speakers in her family. This should include reading and writing in the native language, if the language has a written system. Encourage parents to read to the child in the home language to reinforce the concept of print. She needs to develop fully in English through interactions with native or bilingual speakers of English. Of course, it may be that some family members already speak English and some do not. It also may be that the family might want to practice English together. Remember, though, that it is not recommended to try to change family language patterns. That practice leads to frustration and feelings of inadequacy.

Fourth, try to find out if the child is already literate in her native language. This will have an impact on her learning and your teaching, especially if you discover that her native language does not use the Roman alphabet, does not go from left to right, or does not share many cognates (words that sound somewhat like English). Linguists tell us that of the 4000 or so languages that have been identified, more do not have a written system than do. You may find that your child speaks a language that has no written form and that she has no familiarity with print. Additionally, some languages share more similarities with English than others. For example, it is easier for a Spanish speaker to learn English than for a Swahili speaker. Spanish and English contain many words that look and sound somewhat alike (e.g., *madre* and *mother, abril* and *April, no* and *no*). Spanish adds suffixes to words to change singular to plural (*chica - girl, chicas - girls*) or to indicate person (*hablo,* I speak; *hablamos,* we speak). By contrast, Swahili has almost no words that sound or look like English words, and Swahili uses prefixes and infixes to change singular to plural and to indicate tense and other things. *Mtoto* means *child,* but *watoto* means *children; analala* means *he is sleeping,* but *alilala* means *he slept.* Certainly you don't need to know another language to help a child learn English, but it helps you in your tutoring at least to be aware that when you say to the child, "In English we make words more than one by adding an -s," that child may have no idea where the -s needs to be added.

Fifth, do not tell the child that English is the hardest language for anybody to learn; you may have heard that, but it is not an accurate statement and it certainly presents a depressing picture for a little child. English has irregularities, based on all the different influences on it over the centuries and the fact that the late fifteenth century printers set into print late middle English. However, in the scheme of languages, English falls in the middle in terms of difficulty in learning.

See what the school recommends for the English language learner. Although the experts debate this point, some say that a good time to tutor is during part of the school day, especially if the school system does not provide semi-intensive (several hours daily) English support or instruction for her. It is not good pedagogy to have a beginning English speaking child sit in a room in which the instruction is geared toward a classroom of native English speakers. (Richard-Amato and others call this approach "submersion." It is analogous to your sitting in a room in which only Japanese or Polish or Swahili is being spoken with the expectation that if you sit there long enough you will somehow "pick it up.") However, you also want to be careful that you are not pulling the child out of classes in which she is participating and learning. Again, it is extremely important that you or the program coordinator discuss this issue with the child's teacher. The discussions of reading, writing and tutoring techniques that follow can certainly be applied to the child learning English. You may find that the classroom teacher welcomes your help.

What Kind of Test Do I Give to Know Where to Start with My Student?

This question is probably what causes tutors more apprehension than any other aspect of tutoring. Not knowing where to begin, we're often afraid we'll start with material too easy or too hard and thus ruin the child's self-esteem and educational aspirations forever!

Relax. Think about yourself. When you try to do something new, do you take a test first? Usually not. Usually you try to do whatever it is until you reach a level at which your efforts fail you. Or, if you are being "tutored," your tutor asks if you can swim, for example, or play guitar, or drive. You answer "yes," "no," or "a little."

As a tutor, you will need to ask: ask the program coordinator, the parent, or the child. First, in a program with a school coordinator or liaison, you should ask for some useful information from the teacher or school. It is not useful, for example, for you as a tutor to know that the child reads on a first grade, third month level. What does that mean? It is more useful, more helpful, for you to know that he does not recognize letters or that he cannot read any words by sight or that he cannot write or read his name. That kind of information makes you aware of his needs, and it also helps you plan lessons to address those needs.

If you have no information about the child, start by asking the child some questions:

"Do you like to read?"

"What do you read?"

Flip to Appendix E and point to a few (two to three) of the words using a short *a* word pattern. Say, "Read me a couple of those." If the student does not respond, it may mean he cannot read, or it may mean he is shy and is not about to read to you!

If he zips through the short *a* words, open an easy book (for example, an *I Can Read* book) and ask him to read. Then listen. By listening, you are informally assessing oral reading.

A tutor can find out a great deal about a student's reading by listening to him read aloud. As he reads aloud, listen for patterns and make mental notes of answers to these questions:

1. Does he hesitate before each word?

2. Does he consistently miscall certain letters or words?

3. Does he read word for word instead of in phrases?

4. Does he read with intonations using his voice to denote questions, commands, or dialogue?

5. Does he pause at the end of a sentence?

6. Does he stop at the end of a paragraph?

7. For words that are miscalled, is the problem one of misreading (*cow* for *could*) or one of seeing one word and calling it a similar word (*house* for *home*)?

8. Does he catch himself when the words he reads do not make sense? (e.g., Does he say, "Oh, that doesn't make sense" when he reads "I was so sick I cow not eat my supper"?

Listening for answers to these eight questions as your student reads will help you plan instruction. If he hesitates before reading each word, you will want to work on fluency. Perhaps the text is too difficult for him. If he consistently reads beginning *br* blends (*brick, bring*) as simple *b,* you'll want to work on words beginning with *br.* If he doesn't hesitate at the end of a sentence, you'll want to let him know that a period signifies a pause.

After he reads a paragraph, "test" him for comprehension. You can do this simply by asking, "What's happening?" If he cannot tell you, have him read the passage again and ask him again. If he still cannot, then comprehension is a problem. Make a note in the portfolio. If comprehension is not a problem with the easy passage, move to more difficult material—more difficult literature or content area books like social studies or science. Continue to question and note his responses.

The very beginning reader is discussed in Chapter Five. Suffice it to say here that for the child who will not or cannot read the short *a* words, you can point to letters, asking the child to identify three or four of them. If he cannot, Chapter Five will help you plan your lessons.

Assess writing in the same way. Ask the child to write his name for you. Can he? How does he hold his pencil? Do his letters fit on lined paper? Does he need a whole sheet for one word? Does he spell correctly? When he writes two or more words, does he space between them? Note your observations in the portfolio.

You will need to assess oral language. For the native English speaker, notice the development of her vocabulary. Ask her to tell you about a picture in a story book and notice whether she can identify the concrete nouns (the things she sees in the picture). Does she make nouns plural? Does she change tenses on verbs? Can she ask questions? Record your observations in the portfolio.

For the child learning English, you will also want to do a good deal of asking, listening, and observing. One of the first things you will want to do with this child is to get a sense of his oral English fluency. How fluent is his speech? The child's level of oral English will help you determine how you can go about tutoring him. Remember that there are several stages in moving from a beginning to an advanced level of English. To get some idea of what the child already knows, ask him to talk about a picture; listen to him read; observe his actions — through these activities, you will see areas in which you can build on his strengths, on what he already knows, as you seek to address his needs.

Below are eight activities to help you assess the child learning English. By asking the child to perform the activities in the list below, you will be able to better understand what he can and cannot do with oral English. Be aware, though, that not pronouncing words like a native speaker or not understanding all your questions or commands does not mean he knows "no" English. An English language learner can certainly communicate even though he does not have "perfect" English.

Three strong words of caution: One, the list of activities below is NOT a test. Rather it should be used as a way of gathering information. Relax with the child and make your sessions enjoyable, something the two of you can do together. Make sure the child is comfortable.

Two, no matter what your assessment shows, don't let your lessons focus on too many "grammar" exercises. For example, if you find that the child has trouble forming plurals, you can call attention to them in speech, in reading, or in pictures. You would not, however, want to spend 20 minutes going over plurals.

Finally, remember that sometimes an English language learner may not know a word because he does not know how to say it in English. Sometimes, though, the child may not know a word because he does not have a concept for it. If you have taught the child a word in English and he still seems confused, you may need to develop the concept for that word by providing different examples of it.

The list below is sequenced from less difficult to more difficult. If the child begins to show discomfort or is confused, stop at that point. Then begin your tutoring by building from that point. Ideas for how to work with children limited in their English speaking ability are given in answer to the earlier question, "The Child I Am Tutoring Does Not Speak English. What Do I Do?" Also a useful technique to encourage both reading and oral English language development is the Language Experience Approach, discussed in Chapter Four. As you work through these assessment activities, make sure you write down areas in which the child needs assistance. Include these notes in your child's portfolio.

To assess the child learning English,

1. Ask the child to point to various objects around the room as you name them. You can also have him point to objects, people, etc. in pictures.

2. If the child appears comfortable with this activity, ask him to name these objects in the classroom.

3. Have him identify the following from pictures: family members, clothing, colors, animals, days of the week, months of the year, etc.

4. Have him point to or name his own body parts.

5. If the child appears comfortable with the above tasks, ask him simple questions as you look at a picture together. Use "what," "who," and "where" questions. As you listen to his answers, note grammatical or vocabulary difficulties.

6. Increase the complexity of the questions by asking "why" and "how" questions. Listen for whether the child can respond with only a word or two, or whether he speaks in phrases or complete sentences. Listen for the use of plurals (boy, boys); past and present tenses (am looking, looked, etc.); irregular nouns (men, women, etc.); irregular verbs (do, done, did; go, went, gone, etc.); and appropriate pronouns (I, me, my; you, your; he, him, his, etc.) Again note your observations.

7. Ask questions about what the child likes to do or about school. As you are questioning, listen for word order errors. Does the child say, "a white house" or "a house white"? Remember that such word order "errors" may indicate the child is relying on the native language to help him out. You can gently, over time, point out how these words are normally ordered in English. Again note your observations.

29

8. If the child appears to answer questions with ease, have him ask you some questions. Ask, "What would you like to know about me?" You may also want to bring in pictures of you and your family or friends. Show them to the child. Ask, " What would you like me to tell you about these pictures?" Again, listen for the way in which the child asks questions. Does he have trouble with particular question forms? Note these.

Unless the child speaks no English at all, you will want to use the questions on page 33 to appraise his reading ability, as you would with a native English speaking child. Do not assume that if the child can't speak well, then he can't read. You will need to find out. The child may also be learning to read in his native language. If so, this training will be helpful since reading skills learned in the native language usually transfer to reading in English.

Why bother with assessment? The most important reason is to use initial and on-going assessment in planning your lessons. Assessment should drive instruction: teach what your assessment indicates needs to be taught. In return, instruction should drive assessment: assess what you have taught. It makes no sense to teach the consonant sounds and symbols if the child already knows them; however, if you teach the consonant sounds and symbols, don't assess your instruction by testing the child's knowledge of vowels.

As a tutor, you do not need to be involved in any form of formal testing. The issue is too complex to explain here, but there are a multitude of legalities involved with formal testing and confidentiality. To return to our earlier analogy of a baby learning to talk, does a parent give the baby a formal test to decide where to begin? Even if you as a tutor can't give a test, you can still find out enough information to help you plan your lessons.

Of course, it may be that all assignments for the child will be given to you by the program coordinator. It may be that you will need to fill out forms for your program or help with a formal assessment. Certainly you will want to record your observations weekly in the child's portfolio, especially as one need is addressed and another is identified. These records of observations show growth over time. The program may have a record keeping sheet; if not, suggest one be developed.

One final word about assessment: Every time you meet with your child, you should be constantly assessing. Do not dwell on what the child cannot do. If you see that he cannot write his first name, don't ask him to write his last name. If he can't read very simple words, don't ask him to read hard ones. In other words, simple and quick initial assessment gives you enough information to begin working with the child; continued attention to what the child does and how he does it will supply you with plenty of information for subsequent work.

As you read through the rest of the book, you will find many references to assessment. Come back to these pages if you need to. Remember, too, that you should consult the program coordinator or principal if you have concerns for which you feel you cannot find solutions.

How Do I Plan Lessons and Keep Records?

It is helpful to the coherence of the program for the teacher or coordinator to have records of what the child has worked on in tutoring and a brief assessment of how the child has responded. It is also helpful for you or whoever works with the child next to know what material has been covered, what material needs review, etc. For these reasons as well as for documentation purposes, the program should keep a portfolio on each child. That portfolio, which can be kept in an inexpensive folder, should contain a record of the child's attendance at tutoring sessions, the tutor's name for each session, the date and time of sessions, what material was covered, and any other pertinent information (e.g., assessment of reading, oral language, etc.).

The portfolio, alphabetized along with those of other students in the tutoring program, should probably be kept at the site in a file cabinet or crate. Although confidential information should not be included in unsecured folders, the portfolio provides an excellent place to keep your notes on your student's assessment, performance, and progress. Your program should address the portfolio issue in terms of location and content.

If you work with a program that does not keep documentation, you should insist that a record keeping process be instituted. At the very least, record keeping is necessary to record your assessment over time. It is not efficient for a tutor to plan lessons out of the blue, as it were, not knowing what material has or has not been covered.

Also, as we have discussed earlier, research tells us that tutoring programs working in concert with the classroom are more effective. Documentation—through portfolios or lesson sheets or whatever—allows the tutor and teacher to stay in communication with each other. And if you tutor in a program in which you may work with different children from time to time, documentation provides you with background about any child you may need to serve. Finally, the school, school system, or your program may be required to use these records in various ways for various reasons. Documentation can be very simple, but it is a necessary component of an effective tutoring program.

In terms of your lesson plan, you may find that the school or program has already planned it. If not, each lesson should contain the following:

a) Greeting - Spend a few minutes asking the child about her day. Be positive and open.

b) Reading - Some type of text should provide the basis of the lesson. "Text" can mean any kind of appropriate print: a poem, language experience story, a short story, a passage in a text book, a valentine or greeting card, a menu, a toy catalogue, etc.

c) Comprehension Check - After reading, have the student retell or write in her own words what she has read or what you have read to her.

d) Skills - Using Chapters Four and Five as well as the scripted lesson in Appendix F as guides, do several activities to build skills.

e) Writing - Make sure that some writing takes place at each lesson, even if writing means tracing, drawing, or producing no more than a letter or a word. Some children (and adults!) are frightened of writing, so you want to provide multiple opportunities for the child to put pencil to paper. And every time a child writes, she should then read her writing. To read one's own writing supplies that wonderful reading-writing connection so important to establish in the learning process.

f) Reading for Pleasure - End with a few minutes of reading to the child (or her reading to you if she wishes). This should be followed with a warm smile and a warm goodbye.

(Appendix G contains a sample lesson plan that you certainly may use or adapt.)

SUMMARY

One-to-one tutoring works! Before there was ever such a thing as school, one person learned from another, usually older and more experienced in whatever the subject was. Roman children learned from Greek tutors; Benjamin Franklin learned as he apprenticed; children learn from parents or caregivers. As a tutor, you can supply individual assessment and instruction, you can provide the additional support and reinforcement, you can make the difference.

★ ★ ★

Literacy Volunteers of America, Inc.

Chapter Three

INTRODUCING READING STRATEGIES

- Before Reading

- During Reading

- After Reading

COMPREHENSION

- Literal Interpretation

- Inference

- Critical Thinking

- Directed Questioning Strategies

FLUENCY IN READING

Modeled Reading

Assisted Reading

- Silent Reading Following a Leader

- Choral Reading

- Impress or Shadow Reading

- Phrase Reading

SUMMARY

Chapter Three
Reading

Chapter Three presents an overview of reading, presenting you with information and models you will need as you tutor. Key to this chapter are these ideas:

- A good reader is an "active" reader.

- You can help a child learn strategies to become a better reader.

- A few minutes spent looking over a text and talking about it before, during, and after actual reading can make a difference in comprehension.

- Different kinds of texts require different reading skills.

- Reading means understanding a text; reading comprehension is more than sounding out or calling or knowing the meaning of words on a page.

- A reader is better able to understand a passage on a subject he knows something about and/or has an interest in.

- Fluency comes from reading, re-reading, and reading yet again.

Read the whole chapter, keeping these seven key ideas in mind. As you read, think first about yourself as a reader. Then, think about the child you will tutor.

Children can gain confidence and practice in understanding or building meaning during their reading if they are aware of and consciously try to model what many good readers do when they read. Good readers, proficient readers, instinctively engage in a kind of dialogue with a text before, during, and after reading.

Before reading, good readers usually examine the text, make predictions about the nature of the reading, flip through the pages to see the format and the illustrations; good readers "check out" the text before they begin to read.

During reading, good readers talk to themselves, making sure they understand what they've been reading, summarizing key ideas if they're reading more difficult material, rereading if they find they're not understanding. They also check to see if their predictions were accurate; they update those predictions as they read further along in the text. This "self-talk" can be silent or aloud, but it allows readers the opportunity to check for understanding as they read.

Sometimes good readers take notes; sometimes they go to the dictionary. They often quickly skim non-technical material. Proficient readers vary the strategies they use when they read, depending on the difficulty of the text and their interest in and knowledge about the subject.

After reading, good readers usually "respond" to the material. After reading stories, poetry, fables, or inspirational essays, readers often respond emotionally: We say, "I loved the ending." "I can't believe it ended that way." "That character was so funny." "I wish that story had not ended."

After the emotional response good readers are ready to look at other aspects of the text: "What did I learn?" "Did I guess right?" "Have I ever had anything like this happen to me?" "I wish I could meet _____." "What were those words I didn't know?"

Introducing Reading Strategies

Comprehension

Though good readers usually fit the description above, they often are not aware of what they do. You can work to help a new reader understand why strategies are important and help her incorporate this kind of self-talk into her own reading. Below are guidelines to help you translate to your student the strategies good readers use. These strategies work with all kinds of texts: stories and poetry, for example, as well as social studies and mathematics. Notice that reading strategies take place before, during, and after reading a text.

Before Reading:

1. **Get the child into the habit of previewing and predicting.** Have the student look at the title, chapter headings, subheadings, bold type, and illustrations before reading the text. Through these previewing activities, she is making connections in her mind between the subject of the material and what she already knows.

The child should also be asked to predict what she thinks the passage will be about. You might ask, "What do you suppose is going to happen to the green eggs and ham?" A child can predict by looking at pictures, reading the title, or reading subheadings. She can predict in content areas, too. In mathematics, for example, have the student look at homework or class problems. Have her tell you about each problem: Is there a plus sign? A minus sign? Ask the student what happens if there is a plus sign. If the problem is a word problem, have the student read it silently and then aloud to you; ask her to talk you through the problem. You might ask, "What do we know?" "What do we need to find out?" "What do we do first?"

You can check for prior knowledge during prereading. Does the child have any firsthand knowledge about the topic? If not, you will need to do some explaining, or the reading may not make sense to the child. Remember that you may need to help the child give a name to what may seem a familiar item to you.

For example, suppose you are reading a story about a zebra. The child may have seen many pictures of zebras but may have never realized that there is a difference between a zebra and a horse. When you talk to the child during a prereading activity, if you find that she thinks a zebra is a striped horse, you will need to supply information: A zebra is not just a striped horse. It's an animal that has stripes and usually lives in Africa. If you don't explain the concept, then the word "zebra" will not mean anything to the child, who will be looking for the word "horse" in the text. And even though the child may be able to pronounce the word "zebra," it will evoke no mental picture for her because she has no idea what the word means. The child can not make predictions about the story of a zebra until she first knows what a zebra is.

With an English language learner (ELL), a child whose home or first language is not English, it is especially critical to check for background knowledge or vocabulary. It is frustrating to an English language learner to know a concept and words associated with that concept in her language but not be able to express her knowledge in the second language. It is equally frustrating for any child to be in a situation in which he or she does not understand the meanings of spoken or written words. As you work with a child on previewing and predicting, continue to be sensitive about background knowledge and vocabulary.

2. **If the material has a summary, have the student read it first and retell it to you in her own words.** If the student cannot paraphrase (retell in her own words the story or body of print read), suggest that you or she read the summary one more time and try again. If the student still cannot paraphrase, you do the paraphrasing as a model and proceed. Reading the summary first and then paraphrasing it is especially important with science and social studies texts. You have the opportunity to monitor the child's comprehension early in the session and to plan accordingly. For example, if the summary in a social studies text focuses on agriculture and the child cannot paraphrase the word, then you know that you will need to explain it before the child begins reading the chapter.

3. **Help the student to identify the type of text.** Is it a letter, poem, essay, story, science book? Knowing the type of text will help a student make predictions and identify purposes for reading.

4. **Help the student identify the purpose for reading.** Is she reading for pleasure, for information, for instruction, to pass a test, to be inspired? The purpose for reading will have a direct impact on which strategies to use during reading.

During Reading:

1. **Encourage the student to check constantly for meaning.** A child can learn to ask herself, "Does this word or sentence make sense?" Your purpose here is to encourage "active" reading, the kind of dialogue between reader and text. This is the time to check predictions and make new ones.

2. **In reading silently, when a student comes to a word she doesn't know, suggest she skip the word and read on.** Usually the meaning will come through the context. If not, the child can ask its meaning or consult an age-appropriate dictionary.

3. **In reading aloud, when a student comes to a word she stumbles over, supply the word quietly and allow the child to read on.** The primary goal is comprehension. You can go back to a particular word later and teach it. However, studies show that if you stop mid-sentence and ask the child to decode or sound-out the word, you often stop the child's train of thought, thus preventing comprehension! Of course, you want to teach the word, but the better time is after the child has gotten meaning from the passage.

With a new, reluctant, or ELL reader, you might find yourself interrupting after every other word if you have the student try to decode or sound out every word that presents a problem. These types of readers in particular especially need to learn to develop fluency and to understand meaning; they become uncomfortable and overly focused on the word-for-word if they are constantly corrected.

Don't be frustrated if you seem to be supplying many of the words. As time passes, you'll be supplying fewer. Also, have the child reread the piece several times; after each reading, review the miscalled words and read again. Concentrate on the quality of the child's reading, not the quantity. You may read the same paragraph five times before you move on. Be patient. Fluency comes with practice.

4. Help the student read in phrases rather than word by word. You may need to model this procedure.

After Reading:

1. **Allow for the emotional response, if it's appropriate to the type of reading you've been doing.** You can do this easily by asking, "What did you think about _____?"

2. **Ask the student to summarize the reading by talking or writing.** This strategy applies to all kinds of texts. If a social studies lesson focuses on Sojourner Truth and the Underground Railway, have the child tell you about them or write a paragraph. If the reading material describes a process the student needs to repeat, ask the student to describe or write down the process step by step. In mathematics, after a child reads a word problem, ask him to explain it to you or rewrite it in his own words. If he can't summarize, have him read the problem or passage sentence by sentence or, if necessary, phrase by phrase. Retelling provides a quick comprehension check. If the child cannot summarize the material, then he didn't understand it. You can immediately go back to the text, reread and, then talk about what he has not comprehended.

3. **If the reading is an opinion piece, ask the student to restate the writer's opinion and then to agree or disagree with the opinions expressed in the reading.** Your main questions will be "What does the writer think?" and "Do you agree with the writer? Why or why not?" You may think opinion pieces are too sophisticated for elementary school, but actually we write opinion pieces all the time: "My favorite animal is a _____" or "My favorite television character is _____" could begin an opinion piece. (Another child, of course, might have another opinion; he might have another favorite animal or television character.)

4. **If the student needs to master material for a test, ask her to recall what she needs to remember.** Break the reading into sections, asking the child to tell you the most important ideas in each section. If need be, do this with paragraphs; read sentence by sentence if necessary to teach the child how to summarize. You or the student can make notes or lists to keep for review or future reference.

5. **Keep records of new words. Ask the student to recall or look back to find new words from the lesson.** This is especially helpful with content area reading. For example, if you concentrate on the key words of a science or social studies section, the child will have a head start when she has to read or define these words in class.

With the English language learner, who usually has content words as well as survival words to contend with, this practice is especially helpful. For example, if the first grade class will be working on colors, here is an opportunity to read a book on colors and to teach five to ten words as sight words, keeping them on a personal word list or in the child's portfolio. The child should then be more prepared and more successful in the classroom because of the reinforcement during the tutoring session.

Helping a child learn to use strategies before, during, and after reading will improve comprehension as the child becomes more aware of the active nature of the reading process.

COMPREHENSION

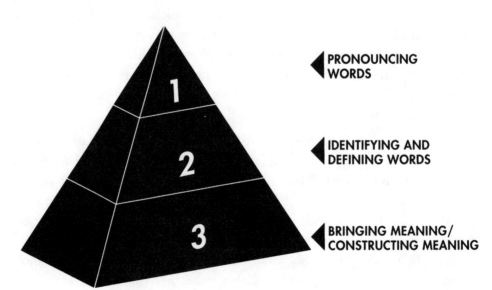

1 — PRONOUNCING WORDS

2 — IDENTIFYING AND DEFINING WORDS

3 — BRINGING MEANING/ CONSTRUCTING MEANING

In the Three Views of Reading pyramid, comprehension or construction of personal meaning serves as the base. As you work with a student, the emphasis of each lesson should be to make sense of what he reads. To help attain that goal, you can introduce other strategies. However, these strategies should be seen as stepping stones to the primary goal of making sense of the words on the page.

Literal Interpretation

The literal meaning of a passage is simply the meaning of the words on the page. Literal interpretation does not include a reader's feelings or opinions. An easy check for literal meaning is to ask a student to retell in her own words what she read. If this is difficult for her, you could ask such questions as "What was the story about?" or "What happened at the end?"

If the student cannot retell the story, you will want to know whether the problem stems from too much material or a lack of some skill that prevents retelling. To see if the problem stems from too much material, reduce the quantity by having her read just one paragraph. If she cannot retell what the paragraph is about, deal with a single sentence or two. If this endeavor is still not successful, break the sentence into phrases by putting slash marks in pencil after words that should be read together.

George Washington/was the first president/of the new nation.

Now paraphrase this sentence for the student, modeling how to retell. Then, asking the student to read another sentence, suggest that she do the retelling.

This practice will provide a basis for literal comprehension of the words of the author. However, literal comprehension can occur only if the child's personal experiences are varied enough to contain similar ideas and if the child has the language (knows the words) to express or describe these experiences.

For some readers, the ideas and concepts, not the words, are out of the realm of their understanding or experiences. If you find such a situation with your student, work on vocabulary to extend experiences by providing pictures, multiple explanations, or demonstrations.

Inference

When you are sure the student understands the facts the author has presented, you can ask for responses requiring higher level comprehension skills. From the stated information, you can ask the student to make inferences (i.e., draw logical conclusions) about ideas not fully expressed or developed in the text.

Consider this sentence:

The boy froze in his tracks as he again heard the squeak from the dark corner.

You could ask the student what the expression "froze in his tracks" means. Did he literally turn to ice? You will want the student to realize that the expression refers to emotion, not to temperature, and that tracks have something to do with stopping his motion, not with trains or jogging.

The English language is metaphorical and idiomatic; its words have multiple levels of meaning. In addition, various communities have their own expressions that are sometimes not understandable to other communities. Metaphors and idioms are often confusing for children, especially children whose first language is not English. "Pig headed," for example, means that someone is stubborn, not that he has a pig on his head. You may need to explain such usages many times over the course of your tutoring sessions, so that the child can comprehend fully.

A simple way to introduce the multiple levels of meaning in a passage is to use proverbs, fables, or parables. Having read Aesop's fable about a fox, you could focus the discussion on the literal meaning (*"There was a fox..."*) and then the various interpretive meanings (*"What do you think Aesop was trying to tell us?"* or *"What could the fox stand for? Do you know people who act like that fox?"*)

How do we all acquire the knowledge to be able to make inferences? It comes from a vast reservoir of information collected over a lifetime. There is no specified way to assure this information base. However, the more we read, listen, and experience, the more we encounter a rich variety of words and expressions, and the greater is our capacity to understand the next idea that comes along. Remember, too, that little children are concrete learners. They need to hear, see, say, touch, and do activities with concrete (or tangible) objects. Interpretation and inference call for abstract thinking. Be patient. Age-appropriate or developmentally appropriate materials provide multiple opportunities for acquiring skills and knowledge.

From the oral language base, we proceed to recognize words in print that represent ideas or meaning. From these perceived meanings and our own inner storehouse of information, we think beyond the words of the text in response to our own experiences. We check out the validity of such thoughts by determining if they are consistent with what we already know. Then we feel justified to arrive at certain conclusions. When we receive and interpret the initial data from print sources, we call it reading.

Critical Thinking

Often people have such a reverence for the printed page that they accept everything in print as the absolute truth. Help your student question the authority of authors when he reads materials open to interpretation. Again, help him constantly ask himself, "Does this make sense?"

Talk to the child about the difference between facts and opinions, stories and truth. Give the student practice in raising questions when he is reading:

> *"Is this something I know from my own experiences?"*
>
> *"Who wrote this?"*
>
> *"What proof does this writer give the reader?"*
>
> *"How did the writer know this? Is he a scientist? Who exactly does he say he interviewed?"*
>
> *"Is he an expert? What do other experts say?"*
>
> *"Can we check this for ourselves?"*
>
> *"Does it make sense that Mozart was four years old when he learned to play the piano? I can't play the piano and I'm eight. I had better reread that page."*

Directed Questioning Strategies

Reading opens doorways to thinking. Encourage the child to think of the who, what, when, where, why, and how when he is reading and writing. You can help the child clarify his thoughts for reading and writing through questioning:

1. Use questions to encourage discussion about stories, characters, events, opinions, and procedures in the reading material:

   > *Which character did you like the most? Why?*
   >
   > *Why do you suppose Max's mother brought him his dinner after she sent him to his room?*
   >
   > *Have you ever seen green eggs and ham? Why do you suppose Sam-I-Am never tried them? Would you eat green eggs?*

2. Ask questions that will structure the student's answers in a concise and logical order:

   > *Why was Max sent to his room? What happened first? Next? Last?*

3. Ask questions that will lead the student to speculate or read between the lines:

   > *Why do you think the new country did not call its leader "king"?*

4. Try to avoid questions that require only a yes/no response:

   What did you think about this book? rather than *Did you like this book?*

5. Ask the student to formulate his own questions. This may be difficult for him at first, but after you've modeled some questions, he'll probably follow your lead. Encourage the student to ask himself these questions as he reads.

Fluency in Reading

Many new readers are hesitant to read aloud. Often it's because previous experiences have been negative, many times embarrassing. The child may have had little practice and may know his reading aloud just doesn't flow smoothly. He may be embarrassed. However, hearing your student read aloud can provide you with information about his comprehension and word attack strategies. Suggest that the student read silently before reading aloud. Don't hesitate to have him reread the passage several times until he feels comfortable with the material.

As the student comes to words he stumbles over, quietly supply the words and allow him to continue. The student who has to wrestle with individual words often becomes so busy concentrating on a particular word that he loses sight of the meaning of the sentence or paragraph. To avoid interfering with the flow of the material, merely supply the word and move on. At this point the ideas are more important for comprehension than isolated words. After you have read the passage and discussed it, then go back and say to the student, "You had a little trouble with these words. Let's see if we can figure them out."

Don't forget poetry, either. Poetry can be useful, especially with beginning readers. Short poems have few words to learn; rhyming poems provide automatic practice with word patterns. Of course, you don't want the child to sing-song the words. However, a poem, because of its meter, lets the child's ear become accustomed to the natural rhythm of the stream of speech in English. Although you know it by heart, read this nursery rhyme aloud and listen to the rise and fall of accented and unaccented syllables:

> Twinkle, twinkle, little star
> How I wonder what you are,
> Up above the world so high
> Like a diamond in the sky.

(In line one, do you hear yourself accenting <u>twin</u>kle, <u>twin</u>kle, <u>lit</u>tle, <u>star</u>?)

Think of how much less intimidating a little child would find reading four lines, as opposed to four pages or forty pages. You and the child can read a simple poem multiple times to develop fluency and then go through a variety of skill-building exercises (described in Chapter Four), using the small number of words in the poem. Sometimes we tend to overlook books of poetry and go straight to story books, but a short four line poem can provide enough material for a lesson or two. And because it is short, a poem allows for quick review at subsequent lessons.

Many times children have their favorite books which they want to read time after time. Encourage this! You can certainly teach comprehension, fluency, and all the techniques in Chapter Four—from the alphabet to sound-symbol relationships to syllabification—through the vehicle of a favorite book. In addition, the vocabulary learned in that book can be reinforced in other texts. (For a sample lesson, see page 160.) There are many positive effects, both cognitive and affective, that come from the reading and rereading of a favorite book.

Below are some ways to help students develop fluency.

Modeled Reading

Increase the student's fluency in reading aloud by modeling, letting the child hear how reading flows in phrases, like spoken language. Even at the end of the lesson, spend five to ten minutes reading to your student. Don't ask comprehension questions afterward. Just let the child enjoy and reflect.

Assisted Reading

Silent Reading Following the Leader

Another effective exercise to help a student's reading is to give him a copy of the reading material and suggest that he follow the words and read silently as you read aloud or play a tape. As he gains confidence in reading aloud, ask the child to read aloud as you follow his reading.

Choral Reading or Paired Reading

It's helpful to you and the child to read aloud together. You may want two copies of the same reading material so that each of you can follow your own reading. The child may join in softly at first, especially if he is not sure of his reading. You set the pace, reading slowly enough for him to keep up but fast enough not to distort the meaning. The child needs to say every word correctly. When he makes an error, you need only repeat the word until the child reads it correctly. A joint effort that doesn't point out any individual weaknesses, choral reading can be a learning experience that builds self-confidence. Studies have shown that ten minutes of choral reading every day makes a significant positive difference on a child's reading after a year.

Home practice in choral reading could include asking the child to read the print of a book on tape. The child can get the rhythm of reading aloud by reading with a good reader, even on tape.

Reading with tapes or compact discs is helpful for the English language learner who may need additional practice with English words. He can hear as many repetitions of a word, phrase, or paragraph as he wishes.

In addition, inexpensive CDs are available now that allow the tutor or child to click on a story and have it read by the computer and to click on individual objects or actions and have them read, too. For example, the child can look at a nature scene; hear the words, *"Fall is a pretty time of year;"* and click on each noun in the picture to hear its name. Some software allows the child to speak into a microphone and then plays back the child's recorded voice. Your program coordinator, the media specialist at your child's school, or your children's librarian can help you locate software. If you are timid about using the computer, you may find that your student can teach you!

How does a baby learn to talk? One way is that he hears words and phrases repeated multiple times by a parent or caregiver. The tape or computer serves much this same purpose and so is helpful to the child's listening and speaking as well as reading.

Impress or Shadow Reading

This exercise can follow the choral reading. Tell the child that you two will read together, but that you will gradually fade out or fade in, allowing the child to take the lead. You might want the child to use a paper marker or run his index finger under the words of the text as he is reading, keeping the pace set even if occasional "errors" are made. As a child becomes proficient with a selection, reduce the volume of your own voice and gradually become silent. But continue the paper marker or finger movements under the words so that the child maintains the pace.

You can get the feel of how much reinforcement is needed, gradually lowering your voice to give him confidence that he can read aloud fluently.

Phrase Reading

The degree to which a child can be fluent in reading may well determine the degree to which he comprehends reading material. As you introduce material to the student, read it in "chunks," or units of meaning (phrases, clauses, sentences). Intonation patterns in your oral reading will provide him with additional "clues" for comprehension. Calling each word one at a time in a kind of monotone is more "barking at print" than reading. For a learner who is reading word-by-word, block off phrases in the materials being used.

Sam-I-Am/Sam-I-Am/I do not like/green eggs and ham.

Use reading material within the child's reading ability. The goal is for the student to recognize how reading flows in phrases and to adopt that pattern in his own reading.

SUMMARY

Comprehension is the basis of literacy, of reading and writing, of listening and speaking. As a tutor, you need to know when comprehension is taking place and how to help new readers help themselves as they learn to use comprehension strategies. Success means students become more self-directed and independent as they search for information, construct meaning, and enjoy reading.

Chapter Four

LANGUAGE EXPERIENCE
- Steps in Using the Language Experience Approach
- Examples of Student Stories
- Checklist: Language Experience

SIGHT WORDS AND CONTEXT CLUES

Types of Sight Words

Selecting Sight Words
- A Word About Word Lists

Teaching Sight Words
- Similar Looking Words

Checklist: Sight Words

Context Clues
- The Cloze Procedure

PHONICS: LETTER-SOUND RELATIONSHIPS

Consonants

Letter-Sound Activities

Checklist: Phonics (Consonants)

Consonant Blends

Consonant Digraphs

Vowels

A Word About Phonic Rules

WORD PATTERNS

Rhyming

Teaching Word Patterns
- Word Patterns
- Long Vowel Sounds in Patterns

Checklist: Word Patterns

Analyzing Multi-Syllabic Words into Patterns

Checklist: Multi-Syllabic Words

VAKT APPROACH

Visual

Auditory

Kinesthetic

Tactile

SUMMARY

Chapter Four

Techniques Used in Collaborative Tutoring

A collaborative approach consists of two or more people working together as partners toward a common goal. How can collaboration be applied and adapted to tutoring?

In any tutoring situation, remember five themes that pervade this book:

1. A respect for the child as an individual,

2. A view of the tutor and the student both learning and teaching,

3. A sensitivity to the child's needs for immediate relevance,

4. A view of tutoring and learning as collaborative activities,

5. An integration of all four language components —reading, writing, listening, and speaking.

49

Your responsibility is to see that the child's individual needs are addressed. What follows are some effective techniques for you to use to develop certain skills within your tutoring situation. It is important for you to be comfortable with a variety of techniques in order to plan child-centered lessons.

In this chapter you will be introduced to the following basic ways to help your student develop or extend proficiency with reading and writing:

- Language Experience

- Sight Words and Context Clues

- Phonics

- Word Patterns

When you learn how to use and adapt these techniques, you will be able to incorporate them into your lessons as indicated by your assessment of the child's particular needs.

Not every tutoring session will include all of these techniques. In fact, you may recognize that your student will not ever need to work with some of these techniques. You will want to tie your instruction to your or the teacher's assessment of the child's strengths and needs. Certainly, address the child's needs as you select the most appropriate techniques for him. Also, bear in mind that research supports an integration of the language components; therefore, it is not recommended that any lesson be spent on repeated drills of isolated components or "fragmented subskills."

As you read this chapter, recognize that some techniques are isolated for the purpose of discussion and explanation. However, it is not recommended that techniques be emphasized in isolation. Rather, if you feel your student would benefit from seeing how a word pattern (or some other technique) may make other words more predictable, you should address that through a prominent pattern in the material the child has written or is reading. Such material is, of course, more relevant to the student than is some isolated pattern for drill on a worksheet. Remember to select your teaching strategies but weigh your choices against the themes that pervade this book.

For additional activities as well as a sample of grade appropriate skills, see Chapter Five and the Appendices. Also in the Appendices is a scripted sample, which shows all the elements of a lesson in the context of a child's reading. Read and re-read this sample to see how that tutor incorporated reading, writing, listening, and speaking and still used the techniques in this chapter—not in isolation, but in the context of a story.

Language Experience

An important element in the tutoring process is language experience. Language experience is a story, an event, even a series of related facts or opinions dictated by the student and written totally or in part by the tutor. Using both the child's own experiences and language as the basis for instructional material is an effective way of collaborating with the child from the very first lesson. This approach gives immediate success and is an ice-breaker in a new tutoring situation. It also gives you insights into the child's world that can be of great help in selecting materials for a series of lessons.

In language experience, the emphasis is on demonstrating the connections between thought and oral language as it becomes written language through dictation. Language experience can be used with the child whose experiences with writing are so severely limited or negative that he needs continued demonstrations of the connections among thoughts, speech, and writing. This technique allows even beginning readers to create sophisticated oral compositions. Language experience also works well with any level of group-composing in which one person writes as the others talk.

To see one's own words written down provides the best of all possible motivations, for the result is an individual's own story. The experience story can be an expression in each learner's own words of:

- A personal experience.

- A procedure.

- Children's literature.

- Content material (science, social studies, etc.).

Steps in using the Language Experience approach

1. **Talk about an experience, a topic from the reading material, a picture, a nature walk, field trip, etc.**

Invite your student to talk. If the student is hesitant or reluctant to talk, take the initiative. Show a picture and ask what is happening. Ask questions from the reading material.

From children's literature, for example,
Who was your favorite character?
Tell me the story in your own words.

From a content area like Social Studies,
What are three important facts about the Constitution?

Or Science,

Tell me in your own words why the leaves change color in the fall.

Some days the story will flow out of the student; other days, you will need to do a little coaxing (or a lot!), supplying the linguistic scaffold described in Chapter Two.

Here is the beginning of a language experience story from a second grade child who needed some encouragement:

T: *Let's write a story about you. Tell me about you.*

S: (no response)

T: *Okay, well let's start with your name. My name is Beth* (points to self). *I'm Beth. And you're Elena. Can you tell me your name?*

S: *Elena. My name is Elena.*

T: *My name is Elena.* (Tutor writes.)
"My name is Elena." (Tutor reads the sentence, touching each word as she reads it.)
And you're seven years old? (Tutor holds up seven fingers.)

S: *Seven, yes, seven year.*

T: *I am seven years old.* (Tutor writes.)
"I am seven years old." (Tutor reads the sentence touching each word.)
Who is your teacher, Elena? Your teacher?

S: *Mrs. Gordon.*

T: *Mrs. Gordon is my teacher.* (Tutor writes.)
"Mrs. Gordon is my teacher." (Tutor reads.)

Quiet and sympathetic listening will be necessary as you discover the interests and concerns of your students. A learner may need time for thoughtful reflection. Ask leading questions, but do not pressure. Give periods of silence: Signs of thoughtful reflection in preparation for speaking should signal silence from you. However, extended periods of silence accompanied by signs of restlessness and embarrassment should prompt you to speak, perhaps rephrasing a question or statement that your student may not have understood. For the Social Studies question, for example, you can provide a scaffold for the answer.

We read about the writing of the Constitution. Tell me three important facts about that. Who wrote it? When? Where?

Look at the following third grade student-tutor dialogue that explains why the leaves change colors. Notice the tutor's questions:

T: *Okay, we read about the leaves changing colors. Now tell me about it, and we'll write it in your words.*

S: *The leaves change colors in the fall because there is not much sun. Without as much sun, it causes the trees to act funny.*

T: *Why?*

S: *It makes a change in the chloroform.*

T: *I think you mean chlorophyll.*

S: *Yeah, chlorophyll.*

T: *What's chlorophyll?*

S: *The chlorophyll is what makes the leaves turn green.*

T: *What happens with the chlorophyll?*

S: *The chlorophyll can't get up to the leaves. The cold keeps it down.*

T: *What happens then?*

S: *The leaves don't get green. They turn other colors because they're dying.*

T: *What colors? Do you know?*

S: *Red, yellow, white.*

T: *Have you ever seen white leaves?*

S: *No, that's snow that makes white leaves.*

T: *So what shall we say?*

S: *They turn colors like red and yellow and orange.*

T: *Good.*

2. Record the student's words.

When working with a single student, it is simple to record the student's words. You may wish to photocopy the page so that you'll have a copy for your own file, for the program, or for the teacher. For ease of recognition, use manuscript writing. Neatly print the words your student says. If the student talks faster than you can write, ask him to repeat a sentence. Your student will enjoy this. If using the computer, type the words so you and the student can see them on the screen. When teaching a beginning reader, keep the first dictated story as short as possible. In fact, sometimes the "story" will be only a word, a name, a phrase, or a sentence.

If your student can write even in a limited way, encourage him to write at least a short language experience. If he is reluctant to write, offer to take dictation in these first attempts. Or you can write part and he can write part.

Do not call attention to your student's English usage in the early lessons. If the dictation is "Me and my doll baby..." or "We done been...," write it that way.

You will want to encourage standard English usage; at the same time, you do not want to imply that a child's community language is not a valid means of communication.

So be sensitive and use your own judgment. If the child seems to have a fragile self-esteem and/or is reluctant to talk at all (and some will be!), you will probably be happy to elicit any words from him and you probably will not want to make any suggestions. On the other hand, later as you talk with your student, you can say, "Well, we usually write, 'We have been.'" One exception is with a new English language learner who cannot self-correct. That is, most of us can hear whether or not our words "sound right." We can correct or change a sentence until it sounds "right" to us. A non-native English speaker, new to the English language, often is not able to hear whether his sentence sounds right, so you will need to make the child's speech sound right if he cannot do it himself. If he says, "Me go bed," you should say, "I go to bed" and write "I go to bed." (You are, of course, supplying the linguistic scaffold described in Chapter Two.)

As you write, don't call attention to dialectal differences or the child's lack of information about the world. It is important not to regard such modifications as incorrect. Also, you may not realize how often you yourself modify a letter-sound relationship. We all hear countless examples of such modifications every day. Every speaker speaks a dialect just as every speaker speaks with an accent. Don't stress these dialectcal differences.

3. *Read the story.*

Make sure your student is able to see the page or the board or the card on which you have written, as you say, "Here's what you said. Watch and listen carefully while I read it to you. Is this the way you want it written?" Read the entire message. If you are at a computer, you can read from the screen or print copies for yourself and the student. Point to each word as you read. When pointing, be sure to use a pencil or ruler or one finger as a pointer. Do not point with your whole hand because the child will not know which finger is the pointer. Say the words naturally in meaningful groups or chunks even though you are going slowly. Avoid "word calling" or saying each word separately.

Reread the first sentence, pointing to each word as you read it. Then ask the child to read the sentence with you as you or your student slides a finger under the words. This may take a little encouragement for a shy student, especially one who can't read at all. You could remind him that he already knows what the sentence says because these are his own words. Feel free to tell him words he cannot pronounce or read. Read the sentence again with your student until he seems more confident. Make the reading challenging but not painful.

If learning proceeds slowly, concentrate on one sentence. If your student learns more quickly, use as much of the story as he can absorb. Reading more than one sentence at a time will help keep the meaning of the whole passage in mind. This attention to meaning helps build both comprehension and fluent reading.

4. Ask the student to select meaningful words.

Help your student read some of the words from his story out of context (that is, separate from the story).

The following story was told by a first grade boy on the first day of school.

> *Batman and Robin live in Gotham City. They drive in the batmobile.*
> *Watch out, bad guys!*

The first grader told the story to his mother, who printed it on notebook paper, writing on every other line. She read the story three times:

Batman and Robin/live/in Gotham City.

They drive/in the batmobile.

Watch out/bad guys!

She asked her son to choose some words (three to five words is usually a manageable number) from the story that he wanted to learn first. She underlined each of these words in the story and he copied each word onto a 5" x 7" word card. (Encourage your student to write his own word cards as soon as possible.)

Batman   and   Robin   bad   live

He chose *Batman, and, Robin, bad,* and *live* as his sight words.

5. Teach each selected word.

Ask the student to look at each word card carefully. Say the word as written, asking the student to repeat the word. Ask the student to place each word card under its duplicate in the story, reading the word as the matching takes place. Then ask the student to mix up the cards and ask him to read each word again, referring to the story if necessary.

The first grader then asked his mother to help him make word cards for other words: *the, watch, guys, drive, Gotham City.* His mother knew he could not possibly be understanding all 10 words, so she asked him how he knew the words. *"The,"* he said "has an <u>e</u> in it and I can hear the <u>e</u>." <u>W</u>atch and <u>dr</u>ive, he identified by initial sounds. When his mother asked him about the last two, *guys* and *Gotham City,* he replied that those were easy. *"Gotham City"* looked "real hard" just like it sounded and *"guy"* looked "funny."

In the science language experience, that child chose these words: *leaves, change, color, chlorophyll, orange, because, causes.*

Elena chose *name, seven,* and *teacher.*

6. Reread the story.

Ask the student to reread the story with you. Be sure to read in meaningful phrases or sentences. You may want to ask the student to reread the story on his own if you think he is ready. By rereading the story you are returning the individual words you've been working on back to their context, the story. Rereading also provides the student with another opportunity to read for meaning.

7. Give the student a copy of the story and word cards.

Make sure the student has a copy of the story along with the word cards for reading practice. In the case of a content area writing like science, the "story" can actually become a study sheet or a form of class notes. It is important at this stage for the child to see his own spoken words in written form.

Follow the program's practice for documentation. Does your program keep a portfolio on each child? If so, does that portfolio contain samples of his work? A copy of each language experience story should be dated, with sight words indicated, and kept in the portfolio. A note here: If your program does not keep portfolios, you might want to suggest that they implement that practice. It is indeed helpful to look back at the child's work over several months as you look for his growth over time.

8. Make and read additional sentences or stories with other word cards from the story.

Just by moving word cards around on the floor or table, the child can make other stories. Our first grader made the following sentences with his word cards:

> *Batman and Robin watch bad guys.*
> *Bad guys watch Batman and Robin.*

Batman and Robin watch Gotham City.
Batman and Robin drive guys.

Here is an example from a third grader in a social studies class. Her class was studying the Massachusetts Bay Colony. This child was reading a book about children of that time and place. She was quite interested in the different educational expectations for male and female children. Below is the language experience retelling or paraphrase of her reading material:

The student said:

Anne Bradstreet lived in 1650 and she was a Puritan and Anne Bradstreet wrote poems, she wrote some poems bout her family. Lots of girls in those days dint not know how to write and she could and so Anne was the first woman to publish a book of poems in the New World.

The tutor wrote:

Anne Bradstreet lived in 1650. She was a Puritan. Anne Bradstreet wrote poems about her family. Lots of girls did not know how to write. Anne was the first woman to publish a book of poems in the New World.

In the course of reading from the text, tutor and student discussed the following terms: *Puritan, poems, publish,* and *New World.* For sight words, the child chose *Puritan, family, first, poem,* and *world.* The tutor asked if she wanted to include *Anne Bradstreet* as sight words; "No," the child replied, "I can remember capital *A* and capital *B.*" Within the context of this piece, the tutor was able to work on several skills: capitalization, phonics, sight words, redundant use of pronoun after the noun (*Anne, she*), and run-on sentences. They learned *poem, world,* and *first* as sight words, but in the process examined each sight word to focus on appropriate word attack skills:

T: *Look at world. What sound does it start with?*

S: */w/.*

T: *That's right; what does it end with?*

S: */d/.*

T: *That's right and the letter d sounds like /d/ in world, doesn't it. Say world.*

S: *world.*

T: *We can hear that first sound. How does that sound?*

S: */w/.*

T: *world.*

S: *world.*

T: *Touch that first sound. Now touch the last sound and say it as you touch it.*

S: */d/*

T: *Do you hear any other sounds in that word?*

S: */er/*

T: *Good. Do you hear /lll/?*

S: *Yeah.*

Family and *Puritan* are fairly easy to decode, to break apart into syllables. Although not pronounced as *tan*, the last syllable of *Puritan* follows a nice word pattern for spelling: *ban, can, man, pan.*

Notice that this five sentence language experience provided the child and tutor with a myriad of learning opportunities. First they sought meaning: Who was this woman? Where and what was Massachusetts Bay Colony? Why was her writing poems such a big deal? Then they worked on skills. In every step, all the language components were being used—reading, writing, listening, and speaking. The word attack skills were taught in the context of the child's own writing and in the larger context of the social studies lesson.

For the child learning English, language experience can provide an opportunity for him to talk, read, and write about himself. He can practice a real conversation with you and practice reading this "conversation" at home. You can ask him the kinds of things others will ask him:

What's your name?
How old are you?
Do you have brothers and sisters?
Where are you from?
What's your favorite thing to do?

As he answers, you can write in paragraph form:

My name is José. I am seven years old. I have a little sister and a big brother. I am from Mexico. I love Power Rangers, my dog, and riding my bike.

One last note about language experience: For those of you who may work closely with pre-kindergarten children, language experience is a wonderful way to support emerging literacy. You and the young child can "write" a story together. You can have the child "write" the story and "read" it to you, though the "writing" may look like lines or waves. If the young child is able to form letters, he may decorate the page with them, scattering them randomly on the paper. The child may want you to write as he talks or he may want you to write and he'll "read" back. He may draw pictures and "read" to you about the pictures.

Make this time enjoyable. Work with the child as long as he keeps interested, but don't push. In this way the child views reading, and writing as a rewarding part of life.

Remember that a language experience "story" may be no longer than "My name is Sarah," or it may result in a child's autobiography. Language experience also provides an excellent vehicle for the child to read science or social studies, talk about it, record some facts to remember, and learn those words important to content. Language experience is a versatile, exciting, practical way of teaching reading!

Checklist: Language Experience

1. Identify an experience or topic.

2. Record the student's words.

3. Read the writing several times, asking the student to read after you.

4. Ask the student to select meaningful words, underlining those words and putting them on individual word cards.

5. Teach each selected word. Ask the student to shuffle the word cards and read them, referring to the story if necessary.

6. Reread the story together. Ask the student to reread the story.

7. Give a copy of the story and word cards to the student for home study, keeping a copy for yourself or for the child's portfolio.

Once you and your student have developed a text using the language experience approach, you may use it as a basis for the following techniques.

Sight Words and Context Clues

A sight vocabulary is a stock of words immediately recognized and understood by the reader. Sight words are learned as complete units, as whole words, though many contain phonetic clues. It is important for a reader to develop a large and growing command of such words in order to reach the major goal of reading—to make sense out of, to understand, print. Learning to recognize and identify words by sight is an essential part of any reading program. Be careful not to use lists of words that have little meaning to the student. The child's own experience story or writing, whether dictated or written by the student, and printed material in the student's interest areas can provide rich sources of sight words.

Remember the first grader's story about Batman? His mother asked him which words he wanted to learn. Notice he chose five first and five more later. The 10 words did not come from an unrelated list or workbook; they came directly from a story he had told to his mother. By working on sight words from this familiar source, his mother was reinforcing the language in the text. Sometimes we make a mistake—especially with new or reluctant readers—when we take unrelated lists of words out of their contexts. If you are tutoring a child who is reading Dr. Suess' *Green Eggs and Ham*, for example, have him choose words from that book. By the same token, if you two are reading about mammals in a science class, have him choose words from that text.

Sight words are taught by having the child look at one word at a time and associate the printed word with the spoken word. Your student knows the meanings of the words because they come from his own vocabulary, from his own stories, and from printed material he has chosen to read or been assigned to read.

Building a sight word (or memorized) vocabulary is a part of tutoring at all reading levels. When a student recognizes many words in a sentence on sight, he can often figure out the meaning of the entire sentence and thus read words in his spoken vocabulary that he would not otherwise be able to read. This ability to note what makes sense in a passage is called using context clues. The use of context clues is a skill that all good readers possess.

For example, in the sentence "I want to l_____ more about kangaroos," a new reader might predict accurately that the word beginning with *l* is *learn* if he knows the other words in the sentence, if he knows the sound of *l*, and if *learn* is in his speaking vocabulary.

A sight vocabulary helps readers predict what words are most likely to make sense in a given story, increases reading fluency, and leads to better comprehension.

Types of Sight Words

There are four types of words you will want to teach as sight words:

1. Survival words,

2. Service or utility words,

3. Irregularly spelled words,

4. Introductory words in word patterns (rhyming words).

Survival words are those words that students need immediately in day-to-day living. These are usually related to the school, the classroom, and the family—what the student needs to be able to read. Examples include the child's name and home address, the teacher's name, etc. (Appendix C lists 100 words from the child's environment.)

Service or utility words like *the, a, and, but, when, where, how,* and *why* occur frequently in written material but are often not phonetically regular. They are abstract and do not bring to mind any mental images to aid understanding.

Irregularly spelled words such as *one, of, have, who, know,* and *give* must also be taught as sight words. Some schools regularly include the 220 Dolch words (see Appendix D). Check with your school's principal or curriculum person or with your program coordinator to see if your student needs to learn the Dolch words. You might check on the child's mastery of these words anyway, since about half of the words in day-to-day, commonplace reading come from this list.

Introductory words in a patterned series (see Appendix E) are usually taught as sight words. Thus, *make* would be taught as a sight word if it is not already known from the -ake pattern. *Bake* and *cake* would then be taught as patterned words.

Selecting Sight Words

Sight words will occur naturally in your student's language experience stories and other materials such as children's literature, textbooks, signs, and words around the room (colors, etc.). Chapter Five provides a list of early sight words.

A Word About Word Lists

Sometimes tutors find themselves in the trap of teaching lists instead of teaching reading. The key is to use lists that are relevant to the individual learner. A list also needs to be related to something and developmentally appropriate for the child (e.g., you would not include difficult or obscure words on a list for a beginning reader).

Memorizing lists of unrelated words—that is, words unrelated to the topic of the lesson, to each other, to the child's needs—is of little value. A worthwhile activity might be for you and your student to construct a personal word list from time to time. If your student is learning English, construct a personal word list from words she needs to know immediately—and remember, she will usually need to say them before she'll need to read or write them.

Teaching Sight Words

Select, with your student, a limited number of words from the material you are reading to be taught as sight words. Six to eight new sight words per lesson are

61

generally appropriate. You may find it necessary to select fewer in the beginning as you build confidence or if you are working with a younger child. After working with your student for a while, you will be better able to judge how many words she can handle.

Ask your student to pick one word. Spell the word for her two or three times. Ask her to spell it for you (supply the letters if she stumbles). Then ask her to write the new sight word in manuscript on a card. (If your student is a non-writing beginner, you, the tutor, can write the word on a card.) A child who can write in cursive may want to write the word in cursive on the other side of the card.

Have the student put the word into a new sentence. Either you or your student can write the new sentence on a piece of paper. Also, you might want to put this sentence on the reverse side of the card. Putting the word into a context clarifies its meaning and provides clues for remembering the word.

Have your student read the word while looking at the word card and then match the word card to its mate in the sentence, saying the word as it is being matched. After she has done this, ask her, "How do you know?" You want her to explain her strategy. You may be surprised at what the child says. When the mother in the Batman story asked her son how he was going to remember "Gotham City" and "guy," he replied "Gotham City is easy. It's got two words and looks really, really hard. Guy is a little tiny word—g-u-y —but it's funny looking." And remember the child who said she could read *Anne Bradstreet* by the capital *A* and capital *B*?

Go on to the next word if the match is completed. Repeat the process above until you have introduced all the sight words for that lesson. If the match is not completed, review the word and new sentence. Avoid excessive repetition as it only frustrates the student.

Ask the student to shuffle the word cards and practice rereading them, returning to the written sentences as necessary. File "known" word cards, and keep separate those that need more practice.

A general rule is that a student "knows" any word she can read out of context at several separate sessions. It is helpful to put a check on the back of the word card if she can read it correctly and then use it in a sentence. Several checks on a word card may indicate that the word is "known," but do not be shocked if you find the child stumbling over a word you felt she had already mastered. As soon as your student can read a word easily over several lessons, that word can be put into a file box as a known word.

Checklist: Teaching Sight Words ✓

1. You and your student select words to be taught as sight words from experience stories, reading material, student's personal list or the Survival Word List.

2. Pick one word.

3. Write the word in a sentence.

4. Underline or highlight the new word.

5. Write or have the student write the word in manuscript on a small card. (In cursive too, on the reverse side, if a student writes in cursive.)

6. Teach the word by telling the student the word, having her look at it and say the word aloud.

7. Have your student match the word card to the word in the sentence.

8. Have the student read the word on the card and put it in a new sentence.

9. Go on to the next word if the sequence is completed. If not, go back to Step 6. If you sense frustration, leave this activity until another session.

10. Shuffle the word cards and have the student practice rereading them. (Make sentences with the cards, if there are enough words.)

11. File the known word cards. Keep the others for additional practice.

Context Clues

You will want to give your student a great deal of practice in using context to predict words. This will keep your student focused on reading for meaning from the very first lessons. With very beginning readers you can use traffic signs like STOP, or other signs like GIRLS, BOYS, or McDONALDS. The context is then the sign itself.

We have said earlier that good readers constantly monitor their reading. "Does it make sense?" they ask. If a child reads a word that makes no sense in the context of the story or if she is stuck on a word, ask her, "Look at that word. What makes sense?"

S: *The grils put on the coats to go outside.*

T: *What are grils?*

S: *I don't know.*

T: *What usually puts on a coat? Let's look at that word again.*

S: *The g-g-girls!*

T: *Does that make sense?*

S: *Sure.*

The Cloze Procedure

One way to gain proficiency in the use of context clues is to use a variation of the cloze procedure for practice. In this procedure, a reader supplies words that have been deleted from a text. This technique demonstrates that a reader uses her knowledge of the world and of language to predict as she reads, that reading is a combination of many factors all operating at once. Encourage your student to predict or guess as she reads. Do not interrupt to correct substitutions. Give time for self-correction. If the child does not correct herself, note what kind of substitution she makes and check at the end of the reading. If a word with the same meaning has been substituted, just point to the word missed and ask if she can read it. If a word with a completely different meaning has been substituted, ask comprehension questions about the meaning of the sentence. Supply the correct word if you sense frustration.

To prepare materials for cloze, any of the following techniques may be used:

1. Use materials easily read by the student. Delete words that require her to use either parts of speech or meaning clues to replace the word logically. Supply one logical replacement and another choice. Have the student read through the activity, searching for the words that make sense.

_____ have fur, and birds have _____.
(Coats, Animals)   (feathers, spoons)

I like to read _____.
(fish, books)

2. When the learner has used the technique described above and can replace the appropriate words from the choices supplied, provide passages in which every fifth word or every tenth word is arbitrarily deleted and only a letter or two of the correct word is available, perhaps a beginning consonant or consonant blend.

This year for my b_____, I want chocolate cake and i_____ _____.
My m_____ said she would give me m_____and let me pick out my
p_____ myself.

This year for my birthday, I want chocolate cake and ice cream. My mom said she would give me money and let me pick out my present myself.

My favorite toy is an old t_____ b_____. His n_____is Boo. He is brown and s_____. I sleep with him every n_____. Don't tell any body I still sleep with B_____.

Accept any word that seems a reasonable fit.

There are many computer programs that teach sight words through cloze activities. Cloze activities require thinking about the text and thus foster active reading.

Phonics: LETTER-SOUND Relationships

Phonics is the one technique which takes longer to demonstrate in a text than to teach. Many children know the names of the letters, but phonics helps students discover the connections between letters and sounds. Many students may already know some of these connections. Other students may not know any. However, if you find your student has trouble with a few or all specific letter-sound combinations, you can use this technique.

As a base for understanding phonics instruction, it is useful to know that we use thousands of words in talking, reading, and writing, but only 26 letters are used to spell these words. These 26 letters are called the alphabet. They represent 42-44 sounds (even the experts don't agree!). Most of the letters in the alphabet are called consonants. Five of the letters—*a, e, i, o, u*—are called vowels. Sometimes *y* is used as a vowel.

Point to a letter in a word and explain to your student that each letter is a symbol. Explain that in English words are made up of groups of letters. Point to an entire sentence and explain that a sentence is made up of a group of words. Note that the first word of a sentence begins with a capital letter and that most sentences end with a period.

Because children learn in different ways that are not always predictable or completely understood, successful reading and writing instruction can often be accomplished best by using several approaches at the same time. Some children seem to learn words as a whole. Many words in English should be learned this way because they do not break down readily into sound units. Other words can be recognized through the analysis of letters and letter clusters. Still others offer some phonetic clues (like a consonant sound at the beginning or end of a word) but cannot be totally broken down into sound units.

There are many ways to teach letter-sound relationships, commonly called "sound-symbol" correspondence. The Appendices and Chapter Five contain specific activities you can use or adapt to your tutoring situation. Appendix A suggests various expectations by grade level. You will find a way that works with your student. The important objective is that your student associates sounds with letters and groups of letters. After learning a basic technique, you may find other creative ways to teach letter-sound relationships. Adapt the system to meet the student's needs.

Children are usually not aware of the complexity of sounds that make up a spoken word. Some students may have difficulty actually hearing the specific sounds in words. This may be due to a type of hearing loss, or acuity problem. Since these types of problems are medically correctable and will affect the child's ability to learn to read, you may need to mention to the teacher, principal, or program coordinator that you suspect a hearing problem.

Remember, too, that some people can hear very well but they have trouble processing information that they hear. For example, they may be able to hear the individual sounds clearly but be unable to distinguish between two different sounds. This is an auditory discrimination skill that they must be able to do to be successful with phonetic instruction. You can address that, however, as you tutor.

Often the child does not know where to listen. Location of a sound is important in phonetic instruction. For example, when you ask him what sound is at the beginning of the word, make sure the child knows where the word begins. Does he know where the end is in the word? The most difficult location is in the middle of the word. Does he know where the middle is? Often we assume that children can perceive the location of specific sounds in words, and yet location of a sound is a very specific skill for the ear to do.

Once the child learns specific sounds and learns how to listen for location and sequence of sounds in a word, she must be able to pull these sounds apart and identify each individual sound. You can help the child train her ear to pull apart sounds. Once she can identify the sounds in the word, she then pulls the sounds back together into a word. This process is called blending. (These are opposite skills, but you can see how the decoding process works, by taking the word apart by sounds first, then putting it back together.) Blending is one of the most difficult auditory perceptual skills for the ear to perform. Use the activities in Chapter Five and the Appendices as a guide. Recognizing sound-symbol relationships, discriminating between sounds, perceiving location and sequence of sounds within a word, and being able to pull sounds apart and blend them back together again are all critical skills the child must be able to do in order to be successful with phonetic reading instruction.

As you work with the child, constantly assess him, looking for patterns. Does he have problems distinguishing beginning, middle, or final sounds? You might make your own assessment instrument based on word lists in the Appendices. Using direct instruction strategies, then, you may continue to strengthen auditory skills as you prepare the child for additional phonetic instruction.

As you listen to the child read, especially the child learning English, remember that he may be unable to produce certain sounds. Little babies all make the same babbling noises. As they grow older, typically developing toddlers learn the sounds in the language or languages spoken to them. There are several sounds in the English language that simply are not found in other languages and vice versa. For example, English has no words that begin with the *mt* initial blend in Japanese. By the same token, many languages don't have a long *e* sound.

So if you are working with a child who pronounces *peach* and *pitch* the same way, don't frustrate the child by dwelling too long on the long *e* sound in *keep, peach, preach, each;* such effort is futile. Much more important for you is the child's ability to distinguish between *peach* and *pitch* in listening. You as a tutor, unless you have had speech training or other specialized training, are probably not going to be able to change a child's sound production. You might, however, relay your concern to the principal, teacher, or program coordinator if you feel a need to refer the child for additional assessment or intervention.

Remember, too, that speakers of different dialect communities vary pronunciation and do not themselves differentiate in the pronunciation of certain sounds. For example, some communities say *witch* and *which* the same way. Others pronounce *pen* and *pin* the same. Still others equate *Yale* and *yell.* Being aware of differences in pronunciation and complications from problems with auditory discrimination can help you be sensitive to a student who does not respond well to phonics instruction. Above all, if a student pronounces a word differently than you do, do not tell the child she is wrong; she is not. Her sound system is just different from yours.

In teaching phonics, begin by teaching the letters that the individual student needs—those identified in the student's assessment. If you have been given no information about the student, you can easily assess him by asking him to identify letters on a page. Or you can point to a picture and ask the child to tell you what the word is and what letter or sound it begins with.

> T: *Yes, that's a picture of a dog. Can you spell dog?*
>
> *Can you tell me what letter dog begins with?*

However, you cannot teach your students to use these letter/sound relationships unless you know them yourself. If you are unsure of the sounds, review them aloud, listening carefully as you pronounce the words related to each letter as suggested in Appendix B.

If your student is a complete nonreader, you may want to teach only one to three letters per lesson. Remember, you'll be introducing experience stories and sight words, too. As phonics work is needed, be sure to keep the phonics part of each lesson short and related to the material being used. Remember that phonics exercises may be tiring to your student. Tell your student why phonics is an important part of the lesson, that to recognize the sounds represented by letters will help him identify new words.

These exercises are meant for those who need help in learning all letter names and sounds. Don't re-teach phonics skills if your student already recognizes letters and their corresponding sounds. But if your student consistently miscalls the sounds of a specific letter, perhaps mixing *c* and *e,* or doesn't know the sound for *k* or *w,* use this technique to assist him. If you find that letter-sound instruction frustrates or confuses the student, you should emphasize some other techniques. Before attempting to teach, carefully study the instructions that you will give your student. In the teaching examples that follow, letter names are shown as *s, f;* letter sounds are shown as /s/, /f/.

Before you begin, look at the list of key words in Appendix B. Notice that the letter *c,* for example, has two sounds: /s/ and /k/. Look through the phonics activities to give yourself a review before you tackle letters like *c,* and certainly, teach only one sound per letter at first.

Consonants

You and your student will be creating a letter-sound dictionary as you proceed with the instructions that follow. Provide one sheet of paper or a 3"x5" card for each letter, using the following format for teaching consonants. Though we start with *s,* the very first sounds you will probably use will be sounds in the child's name.

Action	Tutor Says	Student's Response
Tutor writes *s* in manuscript and points to it.	This is an *s.*	

s

Action	Tutor Says	Student's Response
	What is the name of this letter?	*s*
	Listen for the sound of *s* at the beginning of these words—*sun, sink, socks, sandwich,* Do you hear the sound?	*yes*
	Say these words after me while listening for the beginning sound: *sun* *sink* *socks* *sandwich*	*sun* *sink* *socks* *sandwich*
	Which of these *s* words—*sun, sink, socks, sandwich*—do you want for your key word to help you remember the sound of *s*?	(Student selects word. Let's assume the word *sun* is selected.)

(A key word will always mean more if the student can identify with it. Words beginning with blends such as snake or tree should not be used as key words. It is easier for the student to use a word with a single consonant beginning, not a consonant blend [e.g., tr, cr, etc.]. You might suggest a key word from an experience story, a book you are reading, or names in the child's family.)

Action	Tutor Says	Student's Response
Tutor writes student's key word in manuscript under *s*.	Sun is your key word to help you remember the sound of *s*.	

> *s*
>
> *sun*

	Tutor Says	Student's Response
	Think of the beginning sound in *sun*. Now, let out just the first sound. (In the beginning you may need to say, "Notice how you hold your lips, tongue, and teeth."	/s/

(If the student, within a reasonable time, fails to make the desired response, supply it: /s/ is the sound of the letter *s*.)

	Tutor Says	Student's Response
	Here are some words. Listen. Do these words start with the *s* sound?	

(You can have the student respond verbally or give a "thumb up if yes, thumb down if no.")

	sausage	*yes*
	forest	*no*
	Monday	*no*
	salad	*yes*
	summer	*yes*

	Tutor Says	Student's Response
	Now, lets move this sound to the end of the word. Listen to the last sound in these words, and repeat the words:	

	gas	*gas*
	kiss	*kiss*
	boss	*boss*

70

Action	Tutor Says	Student's Response
	What is the last sound in these words?	/s/
Tutor points to *s*.	What is the name of this letter?	*s*

> *s*
>
> *sun*

Action	Tutor Says	Student's Response
Tutor points to *sun*.	What is your key word?	*sun*
	What is the sound of *s*?	/s/
Student writes as tutor points.	Will you write an s right here?	

> *s*
>
> *s*
>
> *sun*

(A beginning student may need more practice writing individual letters, using manuscript letters or your outline of letters as models.)

Tutor prints capital S.	This is a capital S. It has the same name, the same sound. You use a capital letter for a name that begins with S or the first word in a sentence.

> *s S*   *s S*
>
> *sun*

(If your student already writes in cursive, you and the student should write the *s* and *S* in cursive, too.)

Action	*Tutor Says*	*Student's Response*

(More written words can be added to the *s* page later.)

> *s S*   *s S*
> *sun*
> *sink*
> *sandwich*

You should make sure that key words are words the student can "see." For example, *best* is not a good key word because it does not evoke a mental picture. Better key words would be *bus, baby,* or *bed* because the student can visualize these objects.

If your student learns quickly and if phonics is a review, it may not be necessary to have a separate page for each letter. However, you might want to put all the letters and individual words on one sheet for home study.

You may prefer to use 3" x 5" or 5" x 7" cards instead of sheets of paper. Use one card for each letter, having the student write the letter and the key word on it. These cards allow for convenient review.

Some key words offer phonetic clues (like a consonant sound at the beginning or end of a word) but cannot be totally broken down into sound units.

Use the preceding format to practice the instructional procedures for the consonants. (For Suggested Key Words, see Appendix B.) Again, you should be thoroughly familiar with the instructional procedure before you begin teaching your student.

This practice may seem excessive, but experience has shown that thorough familiarity with these procedures is essential to your success with this technique.

Letter-Sound Activities

Some students have problems distinguishing individual sounds in words. If, after reasonable instruction, you fail to note any progress in the student's ability to relate sounds to letters, instruct by reading to your student, having him follow along using the sight word technique. But try phonics activities at each session.

When working on letters and sounds with a child who can read only a very limited number of words, give her something to do that looks like reading. Using a newspaper or a story book, have her look for the known letters (perhaps circling them) and review the names of the letters, key words, and sounds. This is an effective way of using authentic material at the level of even the most beginning student.

Your student could also spell the beginning and ending letters of a word. Point to objects around the room, such as the door, a book, some paper, a pen, and ask your student to name the objects and then identify the beginning (and later, ending) sounds. Use only items that incorporate sounds the child knows.

Other letter-sound activities are presented in Chapter Five. Be patient and remember that mastery takes time and practice.

Checklist: Teaching Phonics (with Consonants) ✓

1. Tutor names the letter. Tutor or student writes it. Student repeats the letter name.

2. Student listens to the sound of the letter at the beginning of some words while the tutor says the words and then while the student says them.

3. Student picks a key word beginning with the letter. Tutor or student writes the word and draws/pastes a picture.

4. Student produces the beginning sound of the key word.

5. Student recognizes the sound in the beginning of other words.

6. Student listens to the sound at the end of words.

7. Student produces the sound as it ends words.

8. Student and tutor review the name, sound, and key word for the letter.

9. Student writes the letter.

10. Tutor explains and writes upper case and lower case letters.

Consonant Blends

If your student has learned words that begin or end with single consonants, it is now possible to teach blends without requiring any new knowledge. Blends are two consonants in a row with the two sounds blending together (e.g., *bl, cr*). Your student may blend in the additional consonant with the word she already knows. For example, if the learner knows *lag* as a word, the addition of the consonant *f* (representing the sound /f/) will yield *flag. Top* becomes *stop* by the simple addition of one letter sound. *Ben* becomes *bent* or *bend* when the sound of either *t* or *d* is added. The most frequently occurring blends have *r* or *l* in the second position (*tr, cl*). Check Appendix E for a series of typical consonant blends and examples to use with your student.

Consonant Digraphs

When teaching the digraphs (two letters with only one sound like *sh, ch, th, wh*), use the same format as with consonant blends. Note that there is a slightly different sound for *th* in words like *thumb* than in words like *the*. The *th* in *thumb* is voiceless and the *th* in *the* is voiced. It is not important to stress this distinction. Key words are suggested for digraphs in Appendix B.

Vowels

Vowels are a major challenge in learning to read English because they represent so many sounds. Frequently the sound the vowel represents can only be determined by noting the letters that follow it. Note the many ways the letter *a* can sound in various patterns:

> *man*
>
> *mar*
>
> *mean*
>
> *make*
>
> *maw*

Notice how difficult it is to supply the correct consonant sound to complete the pattern when all you have is vowels. Try to read this sentence:

E_e _i _ _ a_ _ _ _e _o_e_ _ _e_ _ ou_, _ou _i _ _ _o_i_e _ _a_
_ou _a_ _ea_ _ _i_ _e_ _e _ _e _ui_e ea_i_ _.

By contrast, try to read this sentence:

_v_n w_th _ll th_ v_w_ls l_ft _ _t, y_ _ w_ll n_t_c_ th_t
y_ _ c_n r_ _d th_s s_nt_nc_ q_ _t_ _ _s_ly.

Yes, when you have the consonants, the passage is very easy to read.

Even with all the vowels left out, you will notice that you can read this sentence quite easily.

A Word about Phonics Rules

English is not a phonetically regular language. Many of the rules formerly incorporated into phonics programs have so many exceptions that they may be more confusing than enlightening to students. For example, the rule that two vowels together usually represent the long sound of the first vowel (words such as *meat, die, dough*) is estimated to be accurate for words in beginning reading books only 45% of the time. For words from a dictionary, this rule applies only approximately 20% of the time. Consider words such as *great, threat, relieve, heard,* and *sieve.*

Many reading systems teach rules for dividing words into syllables with appropriate accenting. The usefulness of such rules is questionable, since the application of the rule often requires that the student already is able to pronounce the word. For example, while the assertion is that each syllable in a word has one vowel sound, it is not true that this vowel is always heard. Consider the final syllable in words like *sudden, leader,* and *system,* and compare the sounds of these syllables with the consonant sounds you have just learned. The vowel sound is suppressed, and the consonant predominates in normal speech patterns.

It is also untrue that each vowel in a word provides its own vowel sound (*rain, made*). Therefore, if the student looks at a word in an effort to be able to pronounce it, he may have great difficulty in deciding which cluster of letters constitutes a syllable. This process can become so complicated that a student who could follow such directions would certainly be capable of learning the word anyway!

Word Patterns

Learning words by seeing word patterns enables the student to notice more readily the relationships between clusters of letters and the sounds they represent. The most prevalent letter cluster in English is the consonant-vowel-consonant (C-V-C). Here are samples of two word families of C-V-C patterns:

get	*cap*
set	*map*
let	*sap*
met	*tap*

Parts of words that sound alike are spelled alike. Children notice that the words look alike except for the one letter that changes in each word.

Rhyming

Before you begin instruction in word patterns, it is helpful to know if your student understands rhyming. Some children have not been exposed to nursery rhymes and may not understand that *cat* and *rat* rhyme. Such students may not know what the word rhyme means. When a word rhymes with another, it sounds like that word in the ending sounds; the beginning sound is different.

If your student cannot rhyme words, the following technique might help. Provide your student with several rhyming words of more than one syllable, then a beginning sound to which the rhyming ending will be attached. For example, say:

"I am going to give you three rhyming words. Then I'll start the fourth word and you finish it like the rest. Listen:

> *colder*
> *bolder*
> *holder*
> */f/...*

The student should reply *"folder."* If not, supply the word and repeat the series. Then give another example, such as:

> *jacket*
> *packet*
> */r/*

Supply again, if necessary, *"racket."* Continue to give such models until the student understands rhyming. The reason for using larger words is that the student is given a greater number of common elements to help in understanding the notion of rhyming. You do not need to work only with lists. Poems that rhyme work nicely here. You can read two to four lines and say to the student, "Tell me when I say another word that rhymes with 'man.'" If the student can't get it, say, "One of these words sounds like 'man.' Is it hill? Is it shoe? Is it fan?" Have the student repeat the pairs:

> *man, hill*
> *man, shoe*
> *man, fan.*

Show him the words to let him compare.

Once you are sure of the student's ability to rhyme, you can move to shorter clusters:

> *ran*
> *man*
> *can*
> */f/*

You can now be assured that the student hears the common sound and also sees the letters that represent these identical clusters of sounds. Often this is a simple task, but for some students it's a challenge that takes many lessons.

Teaching Word Patterns

Choose a patterned word from among the words your student already knows. Use a simple consonant-vowel-consonant (C-V-C) word first. You will take this known word and analyze it into its beginning letter and the C-V-C pattern you want to teach. Remind your student what the word is. This first word is the clue from which he will figure out the rest of the words in that pattern.

The *"at"* family is fun to begin with because it contains a *fat cat,* a *rat,* and a *bat that sat* on a *mat.* Make cards with initial consonants on them as well as the *-at* card. Have the child place different initial consonants in front of *-at* and say the new word. This is usually a helpful, successful activity for the child because it allows for multiple processing on his part; he is hearing, seeing, saying, touching, and moving to make new words. All of his learning channels are stimulated by this activity!

When working from a list, always list the words vertically so that the common visual characteristics are noticed by the student. (The Appendices contain numerous word lists for use with your student. Try to use them as they relate to reading; that is, if you decide to teach short *e* words from a story, use the words from the story reinforced with the short *e* lists.)

Vowels are taught as part of ending clusters because the sound that a vowel represents is usually signaled by the pattern in which it is found. Therefore, learning a sound cluster as a unit (e.g., *-an, -ed*) is easier than sounding out words by pronouncing each sound individually.

The basic approach to teaching word patterns involves blending the consonants with a letter grouping called a phonogram (*-at, -eg, -ick, -end*). About 100 of these phonograms combined with consonants will provide students with many words—enough to indicate the general meaning of a passage. (For a listing of phonograms, see Appendix E.) The context clues plus the consonants will allow the student to infer many other words. For a more detailed approach to word patterns, see the activities in Chapter Five. What follows is a general presentation. These word patterns or phonograms may be taught in the following way.

General Word Patterns

Action	*Tutor Says*	*Student's Response*
Tutor writes *cap.*	This word is *cap.* What is this word?	*cap*
Tutor writes *map* directly under *cap.* *cap* *map*	If *c-a-p* is *cap,* what is *m-a-p*? (If there is no answer or an incorrect answer, supply map.)	*map*

Action	Tutor Says	Student's Response
Tutor writes *lap*. *cap* *map* *lap*	And what is *l-a-p?*	*lap*
Tutor writes *sap*. *cap* *map* *lap* *sap*	And what is *s-a-p?*	*sap*
Tutor reads the whole list, pointing to each word as it is said. *cap* *map* *lap* *sap*	What is the same in each word?	the *a,p*

(Accept the sounds of the pattern or the letters.)

If your student is struggling to understand this new concept, use only three or four words in a pattern. Too many words may tend to be confusing. More words can be added later.

For a more advanced student, use more difficult words from experience stories, workbooks, or any other reading material being used. For the student who understands this concept, the possibilities are unlimited. Many words can be learned, such as these:

sing	*sight*
ring	*right*
bring	*might*
spring	*bright*
string	*blight*

The technique of teaching patterned words may seem deceptively simple. A student may need to expend considerable effort until he sees that words having common letter clusters often have common sound clusters. You want to help the child make the connection between the visual and the auditory. If necessary, make use of other visual aspects of words. For example, write or have the child write the beginning consonants in one color of crayon, marker, or chalk and the "family" part, the phonogram, in another. You can vary size, shape, and/or color of the different parts of the word—anything to help the child make the visual, auditory, and tactile connections. It is worthwhile to continue to use this technique even when it does not bring immediate success. Its power is immense when a student catches on.

There are, however, some students who do not seem to be able to learn an entire letter grouping as one unit. For these students, sounding out separate letters may be a necessary first step. This individual letter-sounding should be abandoned as soon as possible.

If, for example, your student, in reading the word *got,* says *get:*

1. Ask the student to name the letters.

2. If this does not produce *got,* say, "You gave me *g-e-t.* The word is spelled *g-o-t.*" Emphasize the letter in question.

3. If this does not produce the correct pronunciation, write *not* and ask the student to read it. Then write *got* below it, soliciting a response.

4. If the word is still not pronounced, supply it.

5. Add patterned words in a column to help produce the generalization of the pattern, such as:

    not
    got
    hot
    pot
    dot

As your student progresses, the initial consonant substitution is not always necessary because you want instant recognition of larger letter clusters. The goal is to have your student recognize the entire letter cluster, such as *lit* in *little* or *cat* in *cattle.* Such clusters provide the structure for words with more than one syllable. Learning many such clusters provides more visual connectors and establishes the basis for independent word attack.

This method emphasizes the vowel as part of the word pattern rather than in isolation. Most students will find this method less confusing than remembering distinctions between long vowels, short vowels, vowels affected by *r, l, w,* etc.

There are lists of patterned words in Appendix E.

Long Vowel Sounds in Pattern

It is easy to identify a long vowel sound in spoken words because the sound is the same as the letter name. It is often more difficult to identify the long vowel sounds in written words because in English the sound is represented by so many different letter clusters. For example, the long vowel *o* might be spelled as follows:

> *o a*__*s in*__ *so*
> > *oa* __*as in*__ *coat*
> > > *oe* __*as in*__ *toe*
> > > > *ow* __*as in*__ *blow*
> > > > > *ough* __*as in*__ *dough*
> > > > > > *eau* __*as in*__ *beau*

Teach clusters of words giving the long vowel sound by using the word pattern procedure above. In one long *o* pattern you would teach:

> *coat*
> *boat*
> *goat*

At another session you would teach:

> *toe*
> *foe*
> *hoe*

In addition, clusters that look alike often result in different sounds. For example:

> *ew* as in *sew* is different from *ew* in *blew*
> *ow* in *now* is different from *ow* in *show*
> *ou* as in *found* is different from *ou* in *group, young, four, though* or *thought*

It is usually easier to teach one of the sound patterns (*cow, now, how*) before teaching the other pattern (*low, slow, blow*).

In reading a passage, if your student comes across unknown words with spellings that can have more than one sound, suggest that he try both sounds and select the word that makes sense in that sentence. For example, the context lets him select correctly in this sentence: *Mom was sewing the shirt.*

Once your student understands the concept of rhyming, word patterns are easy to teach and fun to work with. Enjoy this technique and use it often.

Checklist: Word Patterns ✓

1. Tutor writes the first word in pattern.

2. Tutor writes second pattern word directly under first, using a beginning sound student knows. Tutor asks student to read the word.

3. If student responds correctly, tutor adds more words in pattern asking student to read the words.

   If student gives no response or a wrong response, tutor and student review possible elements of difficulty:

   a. Student may not remember the beginning sound.

   b. Student may not remember the sound of the letter cluster.

4. Tutor asks student to read the list of patterned words.

5. Tutor asks student to identify the letters that are the same in all the words. Tutor accepts the sounds of the pattern or the names of the letters.

6. Tutor and student make word cards for the words in each pattern.

Analyzing Multi-Syllabic Words Into Patterns

As your student is learning to recognize patterns, looking for patterns in words of more than one syllable within the reading materials can be helpful. By pronouncing identified patterns within longer words, a student will be able to handle these words more easily. The student can check her pronunciation of the word against her knowledge of what word would make sense in that context. For example, although the pronunciation of the *g* is tricky, the word *passenger* is composed of three already familiar patterns:

pas/sen/ger (-as, -en, -er)

If the student should happen to look at the word in a slightly different way, dividing it as

pass/en/ger

it will result in a similar pronunciation.

These word divisions may not be the traditional syllables you find in a dictionary, but it is not necessary to divide words precisely as the dictionary does in order to use this skill in reading multi-syllabic words. Indeed, dictionaries do not always agree on how a given word should be broken down. It is essential for your student to be able to handle the groups of letters that comprise the word.

Using the following steps, try out this skill on such words as *Martin Luther King.*

1. Student looks at the word to determine what familiar patterns it contains.

2. Student indicates the clusters by marking the words with a pencil as in the

    illustration: *Mar/tin Lu/ther* or *Mart/in Luth/er*.

3. Tutor asks student to pronounce each letter cluster as quickly as possible, blending them into a word. Any pronounceable combination is acceptable. Even if there is a slight mispronunciation, student should still recognize the word if he has that word in his oral language.

4. Tutor encourages student to use the meaning clues in order to get a correct pronunciation.

5. If student cannot do this easily, divide one or two words as examples.

    buf/fa/lo

    en/vel/ope

The important thing is to have your student look for recognizable letter clusters. Start with whatever part of the word your student knows. Suggest that he first look for a part of the word that is familiar. Often he recognizes the first syllable; sometimes he may recognize the one in the middle, as in the word *struggle.* He may recognize

	rug
then	*trug*
	strug /gle

Not all words divide easily to produce a near approximation in sound to the word in question. It is just as logical to divide *apron* as *ap/ron* or *a/pron*, or *baby* as *ba/by* or *bab/y,* but a search for meaning usually brings forth the desired recognition of the word.

Application of the skills you have taught and the clues that come from the context itself should allow the student to pronounce the word correctly. It is helpful to start with compound words that are easy to divide (ones that consist of two complete words such as *hallway, upstairs*), or with words having prefixes or suffixes (such as *compound, friendly, reader,* or *teller*).

Checklist: Analyzing Multi-Syllabic Words ✓

1. Student looks at the word, searching for familiar patterns *(outstanding)*.

2. Student indicates letter clusters by slash marks *(out/ stand/ ing)*.

3. Student pronounces each letter cluster, quickly blending into a word.

4. Student checks against the context clues, asking "Does this make sense here?"

VAKT Approach

If learning is difficult for your student, you may want to use some or all of the techniques described in the Visual-Auditory-Kinesthetic-Tactile (VAKT) approach, which has been around for years and has been helpful in many cases of tutoring. Essentially, VAKT allows the use of a variety of approaches to teach. It involves all the senses, stimulating all channels of learning: visual, auditory, and motor. Thus, the student has multiple opportunities for extra processing of information.

Visual

Take a word card and hold it in front of your student saying, "Look at the word, picturing it exactly the way you'd take a picture of a friend. Say the word." (The student responds.) "Now close your eyes and picture the word in your mind. Can you see the word?" (The student responds.) "Now, open your eyes and look at the card again. What is the word?" (The student responds.)

This technique may not work in all cases, since there are some people who do not get mental images well. This capability does not necessarily depend on a person's intellectual level. If your student says he cannot see the picture, you might suggest he close his eyes again and picture a parent's or a best friend's face or his favorite toy. If this exercise results in a picture, repeat the technique. However, if the child says he doesn't "see" anything in his mind, abandon the closing of the eyes technique and simply teach by looking at the card directly.

Auditory

Auditory techniques take into account the sound elements of a word and may provide a clue to at least part of a word. This gives the learner a place to begin in word identification. Say the word slowly as it appears on the word card or in the reading material. Read it in a phrase or sentence to the learner, asking him to follow along as you read. Ask him to repeat what you said. Sometimes the sound of the learner's own voice helps memorization. It may take many repetitions before the learner recognizes the word. In this way, you are modeling the letter- sound relationship as he is memorizing the word or the pattern.

If there is difficulty, draw the learner's attention to the beginning, middle, or ending consonant, which may serve as a cue. The goal, however, is to recognize the word, not to pronounce each letter in turn.

Kinesthetic

The kinesthetic and tactile are really key to this technique because they allow for the use of movement and stimulate the sense of touch. For words that are not too long, it is often helpful to ask your student to use her index finger to write the word in the air, on the table, on paper, or even on the sidewalk with chalk.

If you do the writing, write the word large enough for your student to trace over with her finger (not with a pencil or pen). As she traces have her say the letters. When she has traced it several times, remove the copy and have her write the word from memory, saying each part of the word as she writes. If your student makes an error, cover the writing and go back to the tracing step. Have her continue this process until she writes the word easily and correctly. This activity provides yet another sensory pathway for recall of the word.

Tactile

Some students can be helped by forming letters with the index finger in a pan of damp sand, sugar, or corn meal. The feel of rough sand and the pressure needed to form the letters help some students remember the letter forms and the words. You might also use sandpaper or different types of textured materials to help the child feel a letter. For example, this technique is often an effective way to help a person sense the difference between *b* and *d*.

One way to provide a raised impression of the word for your student is to write it in large letters with a wax crayon on a sheet of paper placed on a piece of window screening. This will provide an embossed impression of the word that your student can feel as she traces the word with her fingers. Another way is to write a letter or word and have the student paste sand, cotton, little paper pieces, etc., on the letters.

SUMMARY

Often beginning readers are blocked from reading and writing fluency by their inability to recognize printed words quickly and accurately. You now have a number of approaches to address this issue. You will find more specific instructions in Chapter Five and a variety of phonics, word attack, and pattern activities in the Appendices.

Throughout your tutoring, check that the child understands what she is reading and writing. Without comprehension, true reading has not taken place.

Don't be in a hurry. Learning to read takes time. Remember, too, that your systematic and consistent work with the child over a semester or a year is what eventually will make the difference in the rest of that child's life. Be prepared for high peaks of sudden discovery and long plateaus in which progress may not be so dramatic. If you feel that the child is making no progress after many weeks, tell the teacher, principal, or program coordinator that a special educator's assistance may be needed. Special educators, including speech and hearing therapists, are trained to address needs in auditory and perceptual areas.

As you tutor, go back to your notes on your student. Review your early assessment. You'll probably find more progress than you would have believed possible.

Chapter Five

WORKING WITH A VERY BEGINNING READER

Be Patient

Don't Spend More Than Five to Ten Minutes Per Activity

Work Closely with the Classroom Teacher

Use All Activities Within a Context

Don't Overlook the Importance of Listening

Pay Attention to the Developmental Level of the Child

THE ABCs

Recognizing Upper and Lower Case Letters

Recognizing the Child's Name and Each Letter in It

Making Connections to Environmental Print

Teaching the Lower and Upper Case Pairs

Reinforcing Instruction in the Alphabet

BEGINNING SOUNDS

Matching Letters with Beginning Sounds

Making a Picture Dictionary

Using Letter Games

Making Picture Games

DISCRIMINATION OF BEGINNING CONSONANT SOUNDS

Listening Activities

Using Picture Cards

DISCRIMINATION OF FINAL CONSONANT SOUNDS

Listening Activities

Using Picture Cards

BEGINNING SIGHT WORDS

Reading Rebus Sentences

Using Word Cards

SUMMARY

Chapter Five

"Let's Start at the Very Beginning" with
June Wheeler Blankenship

This chapter presents a myriad of activities and suggestions for you as you cover very beginning content in your tutoring. The co-author of this chapter, June Blankenship, has been a kindergarten, first, and second grade teacher as well as a preschool administrator, tutor, parent, and grandparent. (She is also the one who "read to me" when I was a little girl.) She shares with you knowledge learned from 50 years of teaching reading to children and working with their parents, grandparents, or caregivers. Use these activities to expand the basic techniques described in Chapters Three and Four.

You will notice that almost all of these activities provide opportunities for reading, writing, listening, speaking, seeing, and touching. Research has shown us that the more processes involved in learning something, the better one learns and the longer the information stays with the learner.

Don't spend more than five to ten minutes per activity. Remember, you are dealing with little children. Be patient as you persevere.

Young children forget easily. So, in addition to introducing new skills, you need to provide time for reviewing and practicing those skills previously taught. This need for reinforcement and review may mean reteaching. Children do not usually master a skill with the first or second or even third teaching. Remember that these children are very young, and some of them will need a little more time than others. However, when you allow that extra time with consistently appropriate instruction, they will become successful, independent readers. Whatever you do, DO NOT RUSH!!

The following list of skills and activities does not have to be followed exactly. Your student will receive greater benefit if you teach a given skill at the same time the classroom teacher is teaching it. Many school systems have an adopted skills sequence or grade level competencies for each grade level. It would be good to find out if your system does and to work as closely as possible with the teacher.

The Appendices are arranged in such a way as to supplement the following activities. They provide multiple examples for work with sight words, initial sounds, final sounds, and word patterns. Familiarize yourself with the guidelines for these activities before you turn to the back. Keep in mind a couple of things:

1. Try always to use all activities within a context. Work with sounds, letters, words, and phrases that occur in the reading material. So, for example, if you are working on the A B Cs, find the letters in a story, on a sign, or around the room.

2. Sometimes lists of words may be used with *listening* activities; the child is not always going to be "reading" a list. You can have a young child *listen* for and *identify* final or beginning sounds before she is able to read the words that illustrate those sounds.

3. Pay attention to the developmental level of your child as well as to the expectations of the classroom. Remember that Appendix A contains a sample guide for grades K-3.

The A B Cs...

Many beginning kindergarten children already know all of the letters of the alphabet; on the other hand, some second graders still need help. Naturally, you will be guided by your student's needs.

Activity A: Recognizing upper and lower case letters.

Most children have learned the "ABC" song before they are three years old. So, some time shortly before the fourth birthday or whenever you find a K-3 child who does not know, you may try to teach letter identification with the song.

1. Write the letters at least two inches tall on a sheet of paper (paper bags cut open make great paper for beginning writers) or on a piece of cardboard; group letters as indicated by the song. Encourage the child to put his finger on the letter as he sings it. He may not be able to do both at the same time, so don't push the child; wait a couple of weeks and try again, again, and again:

Aa	Bb	Cc	Dd	Ee	Ff	Gg
Hh	Ii	Jj	Kk	Ll	Mm	Nn
Oo	Pp	....	Qq	Rr	Ss	Tt
Uu	Vv	....	Ww	Xx	Yy	Zz

Activity B: Recognizing the child's name and each letter in it.

1. Write the child's name, beginning with a capital letter followed by lower case letters: Do not write in all caps. Some people have a tendency to write children's names in all upper case letters, but that only confuses the child when she finds out that only the first letter is upper case.

    Kyla
    Elisa

2. Say each letter as you write.

3. Ask the child to repeat after you.

4. Tell the child that all these letters combine to make her name.

5. Write three words on a piece of paper and ask her to choose which word is her name.

6. Have her match her name card to her name on the paper.

7. Have the child begin writing her name, using outlined or dotted letters on a page. As she writes, have her say the letters aloud.

8. Help her find her name written in other places (on her nametag, her desk, her book, etc.).

9. Have her a draw a picture of herself and write her name under or above the picture. (You can date this, make a copy for the portfolio, and send the original home.)

Activity C: Making connections to "environmental" print (print in the child's environment like letters on signs, the newspaper, buildings, packages, etc.).

1. Use a magazine, newspaper, classroom, etc. Let the child read the letters he recognizes. (Appendix C contains sight words from environmental sources.)

Activity D: Teaching lower and upper case pairs.

1. Divide the alphabet into seven groups.

2. Work with one group at a time to teach pairs of upper and lower case letters. Use only three or four letters at a time initially and build up to the whole set of 26.

3. Do some matching activities:

   • Write seven upper case and seven lower case letters on paper for the child to match.

   • Make a set of upper case letter cards and a set of lower case cards that the student can match.

   • Play a card game using upper and lower case matches.

b	c	d	f	g
h	j	k	l	m
n	p	qu	r	s
t	v	w	x	y
z	a	e	i	o

B	C	D	F	G
H	J	K	L	M
N	P	QU	R	S
T	V	W	X	Y
Z	A	E	I	O

Activity E: Reinforcing instruction in the alphabet.

1. Use sandpaper letters. Letter forms cut from sandpaper can be traced with the index finger. As the child moves her finger over the rough surface of each letter, she says the letter's name.

2. Use plastic or magnetic letters. Sets of plastic letters are available in school supply catalogues and/or in variety stores as are magnetic letters that can be used on the refrigerator, filing cabinet, or magnetic chalk board.

Beginning Sounds

The child needs to begin to associate the names of letters with beginning sounds of words. It is helpful to use key words that begin with different sounds. You will want to make sure that the child has an opportunity to work systematically with initial sounds, so keep records of your sessions. This is a good activity to follow a story because you can choose initial sounds from words on the page. There is an example in the *Little Bear* script, page 155. (It is not necessary for the student to know all the letters of the alphabet before you begin teaching sounds.)

Activity A: Matching letters with beginning sounds.

1. Use a set of cards with the upper and lower case letter. Make sure to have available pictures representing the beginning sound that the letter makes. (Old magazines can be extremely useful.)

2. From the sight words in a reading lesson, choose three to five that have clear letter-sound correspondence (e.g., /l/ in little, /b/ in bear, /s/ in see).

3. Begin with one letter at a time. Show the child the letter in the story and the letter on a card. Say, *"This is the word s-e-e. Do you know the first letter? It's s. Here are some other words that begin with s: sand, saw, seal, silly, sad, sofa. Let's make a card so we can remember that -s can sound like /sss/."*

4. Allow the child to draw on the card or paste a picture of an *s* word on the card.

5. You or your student may provide a card file box for keeping these cards and accumulating vocabulary words. Such filing affords practice in alphabetizing as well as word review. Most children enjoy keeping their own card file. Begin by alphabetizing only by the first letter. Later in the year you can extend this skill with various sets of words.

Activity B: Making a picture dictionary.

1. Prepare a notebook with a large outlined upper and lower case letter on each sheet.

2. Let your student color the letters. Then he can cut pictures from magazines or news papers that begin with the sound of the letter you're studying.

3. Have the child identify each picture, glue the pictures in the notebook, and write the word under the picture. (You may need to do the writing.)

4. The child can underline the beginning letter of each word so that he sees the likeness in all the words.

This activity can also be used with second and third graders in content areas. For example, one topic might be the ABCs of science or the ABCs of your state or of United States history. Under *F* you might find *"flag"* and *"forest"* or *"Florida"*; under *W, "Washington"* and *"White House."* This activity reinforces spelling and content information for older children, and it can serve as a reference for all children.

If the child is learning English, you can make a wonderful survival skills dictionary if need be. The child can see, say, spell, and write the word. If he also wants to write it in his own language, encourage him.

Activity C: Playing letter games.

Play a game in the car as you travel, walk through the halls, or talk on the playground. Take turns thinking of a letter and ask each other to name something that starts with it (*d*, for instance, begins *"door"; t* is for *"teacher"*).

92

Activity D: Making a picture game.

Make or buy picture cards containing several pictures for each beginning sound and large printed letters for matching. These can be used for years if you laminate them. (You and the student can make these together.)

You may find some inexpensive ABC books or picture cards in drug and variety stores; some of these may be helpful. However, such books often use blends and digraphs (more than one letter) as beginning sounds so, for beginning readers, you'll want to purchase those that use only <u>one</u> consonant before the vowel sound.

Once consonant sounds have been taught in connection with their symbols (letters), move to the work of having the child distinguish one sound from among a series of others. Such discrimination is sometimes difficult for a child. Though he may recognize a sound in isolation or know, "Duck goes with <u>d</u>," he may need numerous listening exercises before he makes the connection that *"dirt"* and *"dig"* start with a /d/ sound but <u>Sally</u>, <u>love</u>, and <u>cat</u> do not.

Discrimination of Beginning Consonant Sounds

Activity A: Listening.

Use the following groups of consonants to make short lists of words that are familiar to a child. (*Note: The <u>c</u> used here sounds like /k/, the <u>c</u> in *cat;* the *g*, like /g/ in *gum* or *game.*)

1. C*, S, M, P, N, T

2. B, R, F, G* ,L

3. D, H, J ,W

4. Y, V, Z, K, Q

Examples from Group I:

can	Sam	Matt	pony	nut	tent
cap	sun	milk	pumpkin	nail	tiger
car	soup	monkey	pig	nickel	top
cot	sand	meat	peach	nap	tulip
cup	sick	mug	purple	nest	table
cat	sack	mop	pickle	night	turtle

1. You tell the student the beginning sound you want him to listen for (e.g., *Listen for the /mmm/).*

2. Say three words, one of which begins with the sound (e.g., *rat, pig, milk*).

3. Let the child tell you which word begins with the sound you asked him to identify.

Plan your lesson so that no sound is neglected. You will always be guided by the needs of your student. In the early sessions, you may not be able to include all sounds in the group you are working with. You may need to start with two, then three, and so on.

Here are some examples from Group I:

sound	words to select from		
s	<u>Sam</u>	tent	nut
	nail	tiger	<u>sap</u>
m	pony	<u>milk</u>	sun
	<u>money</u>	love	talk
p	tiger	nest	<u>pickle</u>
	nail	<u>pony</u>	turtle
n	purple	<u>night</u>	tulip
	sand	monkey	<u>nail</u>
t	<u>table</u>	meat	sick
	nap	<u>tent</u>	can
c	meat	pig	<u>cap</u>
	<u>car</u>	map	orange

Activity B: Same song, different version.

1. Have your student sit at the table with you, with his hands in his lap.

2. Ask him to place them on top of the table each time he hears the beginning sound you have asked for. You may use the same or a similar word list as in the previous activity.

Activity C: Picture cards.

1. Using picture cards or pictures without words, select three to five picture cards illustrating each of three to five beginning sounds.

2. Write the three to five letters on a sheet of paper or use the letter cards discussed earlier.

3. Mix up the picture cards.

4. Ask the child to place each picture card in a row under the large letter that represents the beginning sound of the picture name. (Always have the student pronounce the word on the card before placing the card under a letter so you will know that he knows the name of the object on the picture.)

Activity D: Letter-sound activity.

1. Divide a notebook-size piece of paper into twelve sections.

2. In each area paste or draw a picture representing one of the beginning consonant sounds that you are working with.

3. Under each picture write three different consonants, one which represents the beginning sound of the picture.

4. Have the student place his finger on the picture and tell you what the picture is. You need to know that he understands the word and its meaning. For example, if you mentally label the picture *pot* and he calls it *kettle,* or if you think *pop* and he calls it *soda,* the result will only be confusion. This is true also with the child learning English or the child from a strong dialect community. Therefore, if he calls a picture a term you had not intended, simply explain what word you had in mind. Then, he can continue.

6. Ask the student to look at the letters below the picture and name each letter.

7. Now ask the student to place his finger on the letter that represents the sound he hears at the beginning of the picture (repeat the word).

8. Check to be sure he selects the correct letter.

9. Have the student circle the correct letter with his finger.

10. Repeat this exercise for each picture; then ask the student to circle the letter that represents the sound he hears at the beginning of each word. Have the student do the marking independently, if possible.

Example: for beginning sounds c, m, p, n, t

c m p	t m p	c t p
n t c	c m p	n p t

Activity E: Writing the beginning letters.

1. Prepare half sheets of notebook paper with pictures and the last part of the identifying word, leaving a blank for the student to write the beginning sound symbol.

2. Have the student pronounce each word and identify its beginning sound before writing the missing beginning letters independently. (You may need to guide your student as she writes the letters.)

Example: for beginning sounds *c, m, p, n, t*

_up	_oon	_an
_est	_ap	_ent

Notice through this process we have moved from hearing and saying, to touching and writing.

Discrimination of Final Consonant Sounds

Activity A: Ending consonant sounds (use the same groupings as you did with beginning sounds)

1. Show the child pictures of items whose ending sounds are represented by the consonants in the group that you are studying.

2. Say the word.

3. Ask the child to repeat the word and the ending sound.

4. Ask the child to identify the letter that represents the ending sound.

Each picture may be placed in a row under the letter. For ending sounds prepare the cards in this manner.

Activity B: Listening.

1. Prepare a list of words using the ending consonant sounds represented in the consonants which you are working with.

2. Have the student indicate that she hears the designated sound by placing her hands on the table. (You may want to use the word lists in the Appendix or use the same words you used in earlier activities.) For example, working with our same Group I consonants *(M, P, N, T)* we might use the following words, containing ___*t*, ___*p*, ___*m, and* ___*n ending sounds:*

___t	___p	___m	___n
nut	hop	drum	run
boat	mop	ham	pin
wet	drop	plum	train
hat	nap	jam	man
cat	cap	home	chin
net	snip	room	fun

Note: /M/ and /N/ are called nasals and are very much alike except for the place of articulation. /M/ is made by two lips closed (a bilabial sound) whereas /N/ keeps the lips parted. Say /N/ and feel how your tongue touches the back of your top front teeth. With sounds—and especially closely related ones—it's often helpful to watch your mouth in a mirror; have the student watch his, too.

Activity C: You may also use these same words in the following manner:

1. Tell the student the ending sound you want her to listen for. (/p/, for example)

2. Say three words, one of which ends with the sound you indicated.

3. Let her tell you which word ends with the sound you asked her to identify. (cap)

Activity D: Writing the final letters.

1. Divide a sheet of notebook paper into 12 sections.

2. In each section draw or paste a picture representing the ending of one of the final consonant sounds you are working with.

3. Print the identifying word below it leaving a blank for the student to write the letter representing the ending sound.

   Example: for ending sounds *c, m, p, n, t*

Beginning Sight Words

Even a very beginning reader needs to know certain sight words in order to use phonetically regular words in regular sentences. Present these as they are needed. Some of these include:

stop	the	is
go	and	help
come	can	I
here	yes	no
to	in	out

A. Most children have seen the red stop sign at the intersection; ask the student if he has seen this sign. What happens when he sees the sign? Where has he seen one? Tell him that the letters *S-T-O-P* spell *"stop."* After Mom or the bus driver *"stops"* the car or bus and checks the traffic, he can *"GO."*

1. Write a "rebus" (picture) sentence using *"stop"* and *"go,"* substituting a picture for a word.

Example:

The 🚗 can stop and go.

The 🏃 can go.

The 🏃 can go.

The 🏃 and 🏃 can go.

2. Have the child read the sentences to you.

3. Ask him, "Which word is *stop?*" "Spell it for me" "How do you know that *s-t-o-p* spells *stop?*"

4. Reinforce the words by having the child find them in your reading material.

You can give a very beginning reader a real boost of confidence with these kinds of experiences because he can usually read these rebus sentences without difficulty. There are magazines (like *Highlights,* for example) that have wonderful rebus stories. Use your imagination as you work with your child.

SUMMARY

As Rodgers and Hammerstein tell us in "Do Re Mi" from *The Sound of Music,* "Let's start at the very beginning, a very good place to start. When you read you begin with A, B, C. . . ."

You now have several strategies and activities to use with the child who is clearly at the "very beginning." Enjoy your sessions together. Learning is fundamental, but learning can also be fun. Little children are like sponges: they are ready to soak up knowledge. Don't push; repeat often; tap lots of channels for learning; expect success; treat every child as you would like to be treated.

You have read and studied the manual. Perhaps you have been through a tutor training session. If the time is right in your life, you have volunteered your services to a particular program. As you tutor, many questions will arise. That's why it is so important to attend tutor meetings and take advantage of training opportunities. Best wishes in your endeavors. You will make a difference in the life of a child.

★ ★ ★

Appendices

APPENDIX A
Grade Level Expectations for K-3
Suggested Reading K-5
Suggestions for Multicultural Reading

APPENDIX B
Key Words
- Initial Consonant Sounds
- Digraphs
- Short Vowel Sounds
- Long Vowel Sounds

APPENDIX C
Sight Words from Environmental Print

APPENDIX D
Dolch Words

APPENDIX E
Simple Word Patterns
- Short Vowel Sounds
Blends
- *L, R, S*
Final Consonant Blends
Additional Short Vowel Patterns
Long Vowel Sounds
Digraphs
Three-Letter Consonant Blends
Dipthongs and -R Controlled Vowels
Other Patterns

APPENDIX F
Little Bear excerpt
Scripted Lesson
Reading
- Previewing and Predicting
- Comprehension Check
- Critical Thinking
- Reader Response
Skills
Writing
Reading for Pleasure

APPENDIX G
Sample Lesson Plan

Appendix A
GRADE LEVEL SUGGESTIONS, KINDERGARTEN -THROUGH FIFTH GRADE

Located in the North Carolina Piedmont, Guilford County Schools, under the direction of superintendent Jerry D. Weast, Ed.D., is a progressive, diverse, growing school system serving over 54,000 students. Below are Guilford County Schools' grade expectations from kindergarten through third grade, with suggested reading for grades four and five.

103

KINDERGARTEN

GOAL: Students will develop communication skills that enable them to:
1) read, write, speak, listen, and view effectively;
2) understand and apply information;
3) critically analyze and evaluate information and ideas; and
4) respond to aesthetic and personal situations.

BOOK AND PRINT AWARENESS

• Knows parts of books and functions of each part.

• Demonstrates understanding of directionality and voice-print by following print word for word when listening to familiar text read aloud.

• Demonstrates understanding of letters, words, and story.

PHONEMIC AWARENESS AND ALPHABETIC PRINCIPLE

• Demonstrates understanding that spoken language is a sequence of identifiable speech sounds.

• Demonstrates understanding that the sequence of letters in the written word represents the sequence of sounds in the spoken word.

• Demonstrates understanding of the sounds of letters and understanding that words begin and end alike (onsets and rhymes).

DECODING AND WORD RECOGNITION

• Recognizes and names upper and lower case letters of the alphabet.

• Recognizes some words by sight including a few common words, own name, and environmental print such as signs, labels, and trademarks.

• Recognizes most beginning consonant letter-sound associations in one-syllable words.

SPELLING AND WRITING

• Represents spoken language with temporary and/or conventional spelling.

• Demonstrates understanding of literary language (i.e., "once upon a time," variety of sentence patterns).

• Writes most letters of the alphabet.

• Writes and/or participates in writing behaviors.

LANGUAGE COMPREHENSION AND RESPONSE TO TEXT

- Uses new vocabulary and language in own speech.

- Understands and follows oral/graphic directions.

- Demonstrates sense of story (e.g., beginning, middle, end, characters, details).

- Connects information and events in text to experience.

- Demonstrates familiarity with a variety of types of books and selections.

- Reads or begins to read.

GRADE 1

GOAL: Students will develop communication skills that enable them to:
1) read, write, speak, listen, and view effectively;
2) understand and apply information;
3) critically analyze and evaluate information and ideas; and
4) respond to aesthetic and personal situations.

PHONEMIC AWARENESS

- Can blend the phonemes of one-syllable words.

- Can segment the phonemes of one-syllable words.

- Can count the syllables in a word.

- Can change beginning, middle, and ending sounds to produce new words.

DECODING AND WORD RECOGNITION

- Uses phonics knowledge of sound-letter relationships to decode regular one-syllable words when reading words and text.

- Recognizes many high frequency and/or common irregularly spelled words in text (e.g., *have, said, where, two*).

- Reads aloud with fluency and comprehension any text that is appropriately designed for the first half of grade one.

- Uses pronunciation, sentence meaning, story meaning, and syntax to confirm accurate decoding or to self-correct errors.

SPELLING AND WRITING

- Writes all upper and lower case letters of the alphabet.

- Uses phonics knowledge and basic patterns (e.g., *-an, -ee, -ake*) to spell correctly three-and four-letter words.

- Applies phonics to write independently, using temporary and/or conventional spelling.

- Uses basic punctuation and basic capitalization.

- Composes a variety of products (e.g., stories, journal entries, letters).

LANGUAGE COMPREHENSION AND RESPONSE TO TEXT

- Reads and comprehends both narrative and expository texts appropriate for grade one.

- Self-monitors in decoding, comprehending, and composing text by using one or two strategies.

- Elaborates on how information and events connect to life experiences.

- Reads and understands simple written instructions.

- Predicts and explains what will happen next in stories.

- Discusses and explains responses to how, why, and what-if questions in sharing narrative and expository texts.

- Retells new information in own words.

- Understands the concept of a sentence.

- Responds and elaborates in answering what, when, where, and how questions.

- Uses new vocabulary and language in both speech and writing.

- Demonstrates familiarity with a variety of types of text (e.g., storybooks, poems, newspapers, telephone books, and everyday print such as signs, notices, labels).

BOOKS BY GRADE LEVEL

The following are examples of the types of books students should be able to read at the end of the first grade. They represent increasing levels of difficulty and of complexity of theme and content.

Grade 1

Aardema, Verna	*Bringing the Rain to Kapiti Plain*
Ahlberg, Janet and Alan	*Each Peach Pear Plum*
Bonsall, Crosby	*And I Mean It Stanley!*
Brown, Margaret	*Goodnight, Moon*
Carle, Eric	*The Very Hungry Caterpillar*
Chase, Edith Newlin	*The New Baby Calf*
Crews, Donald	*Freight Train*
Flounoy, Valerie	*The Best Time of Day*
Heller, Ruth	*Chickens Aren't the Only Ones*
Hoff, Syd	*Danny and the Dinosaur*
Hutchins, Pat	*Goodnight Owl*
Marshall, James	*Martha and George* books
McCord, David	*Every Time I Climb a Tree*
Menarik, Else	*Little Bear* books
Rylant, Cynthia	*Henry and Midge*
Sendak, Maurice	*Where the Wild Things Are*
Slobodkina, Esphyr	*Caps for Sale*
Waber, Bernard	*Ira Sleeps Over*
Williams, Vera B.	*"More, More, More," Said the Owl Moon*

GRADE 2

GOAL: Students will develop communication skills that enable them to
1) read, write, speak, listen, and view effectively;
2) understand and apply information;
3) critically analyze and evaluate information and ideas; and
4) respond to aesthetic and personal situations.

DECODING AND WORD RECOGNITION

- Uses phonics knowledge and structural analysis (e.g., knowledge of syllables, suffixes, prefixes, root words) to decode regular multi-syllable words when reading texts.

- Accurately reads most high frequency and many irregularly spelled words in text.

- Reads aloud with fluency and comprehension any text appropriate for the first half of grade two.

SPELLING AND WRITING

- Correctly spells, using previously studied words and spelling patterns in one's own writing.

- Represents with appropriate letters all the sounds of a word when writing.

- Begins to use formal language and/or literary language in place of oral language patterns, as appropriate.

- Plans and makes judgments about what to include in written products.

- With guided discussions, revises to clarify and refine writing.

- Given help with organization, writes structured, informative presentations and narratives.

- Attends to spelling, mechanics, and format for final products in one's own writing.

LANGUAGE, COMPREHENSION AND RESPONSE TO TEXT

- Reads and comprehends both narrative and expository text that is appropriate for grade two.

- Self-monitors own difficulties in decoding, comprehending, and composing text by using several strategies.

- Interprets information from diagrams, charts, and maps.

- Recalls facts and details from text.

- Reads expository materials for answers to specific questions.

- Discusses similarities and differences in events and characters across stories.

- Connects and compares information across expository selections to experience and knowledge.

- Poses possible how, why, and what-if questions to understand and/or interpret text.

- Explains and describes new concepts and information in own words.

- Understands the following parts of the sentence: subject, predicate, modifier.

- Uses text for a variety of functions, including literary, informational, and practical.

BOOKS BY GRADE LEVEL

The following are examples of the types of books students should be able to read at the end of the second grade. They represent increasing levels of difficulty and of complexity of theme and content.

Grade 2

Allard, Harry	*Miss Nelson* books
Baylor, Byrd	*The Desert Is Theirs*
Cameron, Eleanor	*Julian* books
Cleary, Beverly	*The Mouse and the Motorcycle*
Davidson, Margaret	*The Story of Martin Luther King: I Have a Dream*
Ets, Marie Hall	*Play with Me*
Galdone, Paul	*The Three Bears* *The Three Pigs*
Giff, Patricia Riley	*Polk Street Kids*
Greenfield, Eloise	*Honey I Love and Other Poems*
Jeschke, Susan	*Perfect the Pig*
Johnston, Tony	*Whale Song*
Keats, Ezra	*A Letter to Amy*
Lobel, Arnold	*Frog and Toad; Frog and Toad Together*

Rey, H.A.	*Curious George* books
Schwartz, David M.	*How Much Is a Million?*
Sharmat, M.W.	*Nate the Great* books
Steig, William	*Dr. DeSoto*
Stuart, Michele Maria	*Angel Child, Dragon Child*
Udry, Patricia Riley	*What Mary Jo Shared*
Williams, Vera B.	*A Chair for My Mother*

GRADE 3

GOAL: Students will develop communication skills that enable them to
1) read, write, speak, listen, and view effectively;
2) understand and apply information;
3) critically analyze and evaluate information and ideas; and
4) respond to aesthetic and personal situations.

READING STRATEGIES:

• Continue to predict based on semantic (does it make sense?), syntactic (does it sound right?), and graphophonic (does it look right?) cues using increasing knowledge of letter clusters, vowel patterns, affixes, and roots.

• Search, predict, monitor, and cross-check using semantic, syntactic, and graphophonic cues independently.

• Read on and reread to check predictions and clarify meaning.

• Use analogy by identifying a word as being the same or almost the same as a known word.

• Use familiar word parts to identify increasingly complex unknown words.

• Note unknown words for later study.

• Retell information from text in own words.

• Use text aids such as headings, bold print, and italics.

• Focus on details of print only when meaning is lost.

READING COMPREHENSION

- Understand literary, informational, and practical texts.

- Read literary, informational, and practical texts.

- Interpret poetry and recognize stanza and rhyme as characteristics of poetry.

- Infer main idea, lesson, or moral in a variety of prose including fairy tales, tall tales, fables, legends, and myths.

- Compare traits of characters as evidenced in the text.

- Compare and contrast characters, events, episodes, and/or stories.

- Compare and contrast poems, informational selections, or other literary selections.

- Distinguish between fact and opinion.

- Recognize the author's use of figurative language such as simile or metaphor.

- Support ideas by reference to evidence presented in texts.

- Summarize and record information.

- Note and chart detail.

- Discriminate between cause and effect relationships.

- Understand and interpret maps, charts, diagrams, and other visual representations.

- Compare and contrast information in printed and visual form.

- Record what the student knows, wants to know, and has learned by writing in learning log.

WRITING PROCESS

- Show recall of visual patterns by using conventional spelling most of the time.

- Use punctuation conventionally.

- Assess own performance in reading by writing in learning log.

- Use paragraphs to organize information and ideas and maintain the topic focus.

- Use prewriting activities such as drawing, brainstorming, webbing, or storyboarding independently.

- Revise by adding detail for elaboration.

- Mark incorrect spelling.

- Edit to verify and self-correct spelling.

- Experiment to vary word order in sentences.

- Use concepts of order and time writing.

- Critique books in reading log/response journal by discussing what makes a good book or why a particular author or genre is preferred.

COMPOSING PRODUCTS

- Write literary, informational, and practical texts to convey meaning, to learn, and to clarify thinking.

- Write using characters, setting, problem, and solution.

- Explain in writing the main idea, lesson, or moral of a selection.

- Write a variety of poetry and prose including fairy tales and personal narratives.

- Write practical texts such as news articles, recipes, directions, and interviews.

- Write to support ideas with reference to evidence presented in text.

- Express meaning inferred from text.

BOOKS BY GRADE LEVEL

The following are examples of the types of books students should be able to read at the end of the third grade. They represent increasing levels of difficulty and of complexity of theme and content.

Grade 3

Atwater, Richard and Florence	*Mr. Popper's Penguins*
Baylor, Byrd	*Hawk, I'm Your Brother*
Cleary, Beverly	*Ramona* books
Cohen, Barbara	*Molly's Pilgrim*
Cole, Johanna	*The Magic School Bus Inside the Earth*
Flournoy, Valerie	*The Patchwork Quilt*
Fritz, Jean	*What's the Big Idea, Ben Franklin*
Gardiner, John Reynolds	*Stone Fox*
Heide, Florence Parry and Gilliland, Judith Heide	*The Day of Ahmed's Secret*

Hurtwitz, Johanna	*Class Clown*
Johnston, Tony	*Yonder*
Lobel, Arnold	*Fables*
McKissack, Patricia	*Mirandy and Brother Wind*
Prelutsky, Jack	*The New Kid on the Block*
Steptoe, John	*Mufaro's Beautiful Daughters*
Warner, Gertrude C.	*The Boxcar Children* books
Wilder, Laura I.	*Little House on the Prairie;* *Little House in the Big Woods*
Williams, Margery	*The Velveteen Rabbit*
Young, Ed	*Lon Po Po: A Red Riding Hood Story from China*

BOOKS BY GRADE LEVEL

The following are examples of the types of books students should be able to read at the end of the fourth grade. They represent increasing levels of difficulty and of complexity of theme and content.

Grade 4

Boyd, Sandy Dawson	*Circle of Gold*
Chase, Richard	*Grandfather Tales; The Jack Tales*
Dahl, Ronald	*James and the Giant Peach* *The Fantastic Mr. Fox*
Fleishman, Sid	*The Whipping Boy*
Gaylor, Byrd	*I'm in Charge of Celebrations*
Howe, Deborah and James	*Bunnicula*
MacLachlan, Patricia	*Sarah, Plain and Tall*
Mathis, Sharon	*The Hundred Penny Box*
Moss, Jeff	*The Glass Jar; The Other Side of the Door*
Pidgeon, Jack and Wooley, Marilyn	*Earthworms*
Rockwell, Thomas	*How to Eat Fried Worms*
Rylant, Cynthia	*Every Living Thing*

113

Schieszka, Jon	*Knights of the Kitchen Table*
Sobol, Donald	*Encyclopedia Brown books*
White, E.B.	*Charlotte's Web*
Wilder, Laura I.	*By the Shores of Silver Lake*
Yasima, Taro	*Crow Boy*

BOOKS BY GRADE LEVEL

The following are examples of the types of books students should be able to read at the end of the fifth grade. They represent increasing levels of difficulty and of complexity of theme and content.

Grade 5

Armstrong, William H.	*Sounder*
Burnett, Frances H.	*The Secret Garden*
Cleary, Beverly	*Dear Mr. Henshaw*
Coerr, Mildred	*Sadako and the Thousand Paper Cranes*
Dodge, Mary Mapes	*Hans Brinker*
Henry, Marguerite	*Misty of Chincoteague*
L'Engle, Madeleine	*A Wrinkle in Time*
Lewis, C.S.	*The Lion, the Witch, and the Wardrobe* *The Voyage of the Dawn Treader*
Lowry, Lois	*Number the Stars*
Sacher, Louis	*There's a Boy in the Girl's Bathroom*
Smith, Doris B.	*A Taste of Blackberries*
Swan, Robert	*Destination Antarctica*
Turner, Ann	*Dakota Dugout*
White, E.B.	*The Trumpet of the Swans*

A BAKER'S DOZEN: SUGGESTIONS FOR
MULTICULTURAL READING

Bringing the Rain to Kapititi Plain. Verna Aardema. Dial, 1981

The Patchwork Quilt. Valerie Flournoy. 1985

Flossie and the Fox. Patricia McKissack. 1986

Not So Fast Songolo. Niki Daly. 1987

Spin a Soft Black Song. Nikki Giovanni. 1985

The People Could Fly: American Black Folktales. Virginia Hamilton. 1985

Marching to Freedom: The Story of Martin Luther King, Jr. Joyce Milton. 1987

Sadako and the Thousand Paper Cranes. Eleanor Coerr. 1979

The Happy Funeral. Eve Bunting. 1982

Where the Buffaloes Begin. Olaf Baker. 1985

Felita. Nicholasa Mohr. 1979

Hello Amigos! Tricia Brown. 1986

The Pancake: An Old Norwegian Folk Tale. Lorinda Bryan Cauley. 1988

Appendix B

SUGGESTED KEY WORDS

As you use phonics, keep these three items in mind:

1. Teach only the letter-sound relationships each individual student needs, those identified in the student's assessment.

2. Suggest as possible key words those to which the student can best relate. Ask the student to pick the key word.

3. Remember that English is not a phonetically regular language. Some consonants and all vowels have more than one sound or may behave irregularly.

For example, the letter *c* has the /k/ sound (e.g., *corn, camera*) but it also has the /s/ sound (e.g., ceiling, city). Also, the letter *k* has no sound in *knife, know,* etc.

INITIAL CONSONANT SOUNDS

B	bus, baby, ball, bed, banana, bird
C	cat, cup, can, cake, comb, car
***C**	cigar, city, cent, celery
D	dog, dish, doll, desk
F	fish, fan, fire, feet, fork
G	gas, girl, game, gate
***G**	gem, gentleman, giraffe
H	hand, hat, house, ham, horn
J	jar, jacket, jug, jeep, jack-in-the box
K	key, kite, king, kangeroo
L	lamp, leaf, ladder, lion
M	man, match, monkey, milk, mother
N	name, nose, nail, needle
P	pot, pan, pig, pants, piano, pumpkin

Q (QU)	quarter, queen, quilt, quick
R	rat, radio, rocket, rope, rabbit, red
S	sun, sink, socks, sandwich
T	telephone, towel, table, turtle, turkey
V	valentine, violin, van
W	window, wing, wig, watch, wagon, water
Y	yellow, yarn, yo-yo, yardstick
Z	zipper, zebra, zoo

DIGRAPHS

CH	church, chair, children, chain, chicken
*CH	cholesterol, chemical, choir
*CH	chute, chauffeur
PH	phone, photo, pharmacy
SH	shoe, ship, shower, shovel
TH	thumb, thank, theater, thorn, thread
*TH	this, the, them, these
WH	wheel, whale, white, whistle

SHORT VOWEL SOUNDS

A	apple, ant, alligator, astronaut, arrow
E	elephant, egg, elf
I	igloo, insect, iguana
O	octopus, olive, ox, ostrich
U	umbrella, umpire, underwear

117

LONG VOWEL SOUNDS

A	ape, angel
E	eel, evening
I	I, ice, icicle
O	open, ocean, opal, over
U	Utah, user, unicorn

* teach later

Appendix C
SIGHT WORDS FROM ENVIRONMENTAL PRINT

It is never too early to call attention to those words that surround the child both in and out of school. Teach them as sight words. Call attention to the words when you are with the child in the hall, in the classroom, in the media center. You might also want to share this list with the child's parent or guardian. Feel free to add additional words peculiar to your particular community (stores, natural resources, etc.).

Age	Crayons	Found
Birthday	Danger	Free
Bottom	Date	Girls
Boys	Desk	Go
Brother	Don't Walk	Gym
Buses Only	Don't Talk	Help
Bus Stop	Do Not Enter	Help Wanted
Cafeteria	Down	Home
Car Rider	Elevator	Hospital
Caution	Emergency Exit	In
Children Crossing	Entrance	Information
	Exit	Keep Closed
Children Playing	Father	Keep Off
	Fire	Left
Church	Fire Escape	Library
Color	Fire Extinguisher	Light

119

Lost

Mark

Markers

Media Center

Men

Men Working

Month

Mother

Name

Newspaper

Next

No

No Diving

No Dogs Allowed

No Swimming

No U-Turn

Nurse

Off

Office

Open

On

Open Door

Out

Out of Order

Other Door

Park

Pedestrians

Playground

Poison

Police

Post Office

Pull

Push

Rest Rooms

Rest Stop

Right

Room

Safe Place

School

School Bus

Shallow Water

Sister

Slippery

Stairway

Step Down

Stop

Street

Taxi

Telephone

Television

Thin Ice

Today

Top

Town (child's town)

Up

Use Other Door

Wait

Walk

Warning

Watch Your Step

Wet Paint

Women

Year

Yes

Zoo

_____

_____

Appendix D
A BASIC SIGHT VOCABULARY OF 220 WORDS BY DOLCH

a	at	brown	do	first
about	ate	but	does	five
after	away	buy	done	fly
again	be	by	don't	for
all	because	call	down	found
always	been	came	draw	four
am	before	can	drink	from
an	best	carry	eat	full
and	better	clean	eight	funny
any	big	cold	every	gave
are	black	come	fall	get
around	blue	could	far	give
as	bottle	cut	fast	go
ask	bring	did	find	goes

going	how	light	new	own
good	hurt	like	no	pick
got	I	little	not	play
green	if	live	now	please
grow	in	long	of	pretty
had	into	look	off	pull
has	is	made	old	put
have	it	make	on	ran
he	its	many	once	read
help	jump	may	one	red
her	just	me	only	ride
here	keep	much	open	right
him	kind	must	or	round
his	know	my	our	run
hold	laugh	myself	out	said
hot	let	never	over	saw

say	take	to	wash	would
see	tell	today	we	write
seven	ten	together	well	yellow
shall	thank	too	went	yes
she	that	try	were	you
show	the	two	what	your
sing	their	under	when	
sit	them	up	where	
six	then	upon	which	
sleep	there	us	white	
small	these	use	who	
so	they	very	why	
some	think	walk	will	
soon	this	want	wish	
start	those	warm	with	
stop	three	was	work	

Appendix E

These word patterns are arranged in an order that goes from simple to more difficult. Notice, for example, that the long vowels do not follow the short vowels. That is because the long vowels are taught much later in many school systems. Notice also that these patterns often call for listening exercises as well as reading exercises. Refer to Chapter Five as you work through these pages.

I. SIMPLE WORD PATTERNS

The simple words in the lists below follow the consonant-vowel-consonant pattern.

SHORT A SOUNDS

-ab	-ad	-ag	-am	-an
cab	ad	bag	am	an
dab	bad	gag	dam	ban
jab	dad	rag	ham	can
lab	had	sag	Pam	fan
tab	mad	tag	Sam	man
	sad	wag	pan	ran

-ap	-at	-ax
cap	at	ax
gap	bat	wax
lap	cat	tax
map	fat	
nap	mat	
rap	pat	
tap	rat	
	sat	
	vat	

SHORT E SOUNDS

-et	-ed	-en	-eg
bet	bed	den	beg
get	fed	hen	egg
jet	led	men	keg
let	red	pen	leg
met	wed	ten	peg
net			
pet			
set			
wet			

125

yet

SHORT I SOUNDS

-ib	-id	-ig	-im	-in
bib	bid	big	dim	in
fib	did	dig	him	bin
rib	hid	fig	rim	fin
	kid	jig		pin
	lid	pig		tin
	rid	wig		win

-ip	-it	-ix
dip	it	fix
hip	bit	mix
lip	fit	six

SHORT O SOUNDS

-ob	-od	-og	-on	-ot
cob	cod	bog	on	cot
gob	God	dog	don	dot
job	nod	fog	non	got
rob	pod	hog	yon	hot
mob	rod	jog		not
sob	sod	log		pot

SHORT U SOUNDS

-ub	-ud	-ug	-um	-un
cub	bud	bug	bum	bun
dub	cud	dug	gum	fun
hub	dud	hug	hum	gun
nub	mud	jug	mum	nun
rub		rug	sum	run
tub		tug		sun

-ut	-up	-us
but	up	us
cut	cup	bus
gut	pup	
hut	sup	
nut		
rut		

II. BLENDS.

Here are some common elementary level words that illustrate consonant blends. As explained in Chapter Five, you can use these for listening exercises as well as for reading.

INITIAL CONSONANT + L or R

bl-	br-	cl-	cr-
blue	brag	clap	crab
black	brat	clam	crayon
block	bread	clip	crow
blank	broke	close	crown
bled	brush	clown	crook
blow	brown	clash	crash
bloom	brook	clang	

fl-	fr-	gl-	gr-
flab	frog	glad	green
flag	from	gland	grass
flat	frame	glass	grape
flap	frown	glove	grow
flame	Frank	glow	grew
fly	free	glue	groom
flow	fresh	globe	ground
float	fruit	glance	graze

pl-	pr-	tr-	dr-
plate	print	tree	draw
plant	prop	train	dress
plug	pray	trim	drum
plot	prowl	tray	drink
play	pretty	true	droop
plow	prince	try	drop
plan	prize	trunk	drive
plum	pretzel	trade	dragon

S BLENDS

sc-	sn-	st-	sk-	sl-
scar	snow	star	sky	sled
score	snail	stop	skin	slip
scat	snake	stack	skip	slap
scan	snap	stamp	skunk	slow
scatter	snack	step	skill	slide

sm-	sp-	sq-	sw-
smile	spoon	square	swat
smack	spool	squirrel	swing
small	spot	squirt	sweep
smell	spat	squint	swell
smoke	spin	squash	sweet

129

FINAL CONSONANT BLENDS
GROUP I

-st	-nd	-ng	_-mp	-ck
rest	band	ring	jump	luck
nest	hand	sing	pump	duck
must	sand	hang	lamp	buck
rust	mend	bang	damp	back
dust	send	swing	stump	pack
crust	lend	sting	stamp	sack
last	bland	bring	chomp	black
blast	brand	thing	clamp	block

GROUP II

-lk	-nt	-sk	-nk	-ld
talk	rent	ask	bank	cold
walk	sent	bask	sank	bold
milk	went	task	blank	hold
balk	mint	risk	thank	told
chalk	hunt	disk	stink	sold

GROUP III

-sp	-rk	-ft	-lt	-pt
gasp	work	lift	colt	slept
wasp	fork	sift	salt	swept
grasp	pork	left	felt	wept
clasp	park	raft	melt	kept
crisp	bark	draft	belt	crept

III. ADDITIONAL SHORT VOWEL PATTERNS

These patterns illustrate short vowels in a context of initial and/or final consonant blends and diagraphs.

SHORT A SOUNDS

-ab	-ad	-ag	-am	-an
blab	clad	brag	clam	clan
flab	glad	drag	slam	plan
slab	shad	flag	swam	scan

-ap		-at		-ath
chap	slap	brat	slat	bath
clap	snap	chat	scat	
flap	trap	flat	that	-ax
				flax

-ack	-amp	-and	-ang	-ank
back	camp	and	bang	bank
pack	damp	band	fang	Hank
rack	lamp	hand	gang	rank
sack	ramp	land	hang	sank
black	champ	sand	rang	tank
crack	clamp	brand	sang	yank
track	cramp	grand	tang	blank

-ash	-asp	-ass	-ast	-atch
cash	asp	bass	cast	catch
mash	gasp	lass	fast	latch
rash	hasp	mass	last	match
sash	rasp	pass	past	patch
clash	clasp	brass	vast	batch
smash	grasp	grass	blast	hatch

SHORT E SOUNDS

-ed	-en	-ell	-end	-ent
bled	glen	bell	end	bent
fled	then	fell	bend	dent
sled	when	sell	lend	lent
shed		tell	mend	rent
sped		well	send	sent
		yell	blend	tent
		shell	spend	went
		smell	trend	spent

-est	-eck	-elf	-elp	-ess
best	deck	elf	help	less
nest	heck	self	yelp	mess
pest	neck	shelf		bless
rest	peck			chess
test	check	-elt	-ept	dress
vest	speck	belt	kept	
west		felt	wept	
chest		melt		
crest				
quest				

SHORT I SOUNDS

-ib	-id	-ig	-im	-in
crib	grid	swig	skim	chin
glib	skid	twig	slim	shin
	slid		trim	thin
			whim	grin

-ip	-it	-ick	-ift	-ilk
chip	grit	kick	gift	milk
slip	skit	lick	lift	silk
flip	flit	nick	rift	
ship	slit	pick	sift	
grip	spit	sick	drift	
hip		tick		
tip		wick		

-ill	-ing	-ink	-int	-ive
bill	bing	ink	hint	give
fill	ring	pink	mint	live
hill	sing	sink	tint	
kill	wing	wink	flint	
mill	sting	link	lint	
pill	bring	stink	squint	
till	thing	slink		

-ish	-iss	-ist	-inch	-itch
dish	hiss	fist	inch	itch
fish	kiss	list	cinch	ditch
wish	miss	mist	pinch	pitch
			flinch	witch

SHORT O SOUNDS

-ob	-od	-og	-ot
blob	clod	clog	blot
slob	plod	frog	clot
snob	shod	smog	plot

-ock	-ong
clock	wrong
flock	strong
crock	throng
frock	prong
shock	
smock	
stock	

SHORT U SOUNDS

-ub	-ud	-ug	-um	-un
club	stud	chug	glum	shun
grub	thud	thug	slum	spun
stub		plug	drum	stun
		slug	scum	

-us	-ut	snug	chum	-uzz
plus	shut			buzz
thus	strut			fuzz

-uck	-uff	-ull	-ump	-ung
buck	buff	cull	bump	hung
duck	cuff	dull	dump	lung
luck	huff	gull	jump	rung
muck	muff	hull	lump	sung

-unk	-ush	-usk	-ust	-unch
bunk	gush	dusk	bust	bunch
dunk	hush	husk	dust	lunch
hunk	lush	tusk	just	punch
junk	mush		must	munch
sunk	rush		rust	hunch

IV. THE LONG VOWELS

LONG A SOUNDS

-ace	-ade	-age	-ale	-ame
face	fade	age	dale	came
lace	made	cage	male	fame
pace	wade	page	pale	game
race	grade	rage	sale	name
brace	trade	sage	tale	same
place	shade	wage	whale	tame
space	spade	stage		blame
				frame

-ane	-ape	-ase	-ate
cane	ape	base	ate
lane	cape	case	date
mane	gape	vase	gate
pane	nape	chase	hate
sane	tape		late
vane	drape		rate
wane	grape		crate
crane	shape		grate

-ave	-aze	-aste	-aid	-ail
cave	daze	baste	aid	ail
gave	faze	haste	laid	fail
pave	gaze	paste	maid	hail
rave	haze	taste	paid	jail
save	maze	waste	raid	mail
wave	raze			nail
brave	blaze			pail
crave	glaze	-ait	-aint	rail
grave	graze	bait	faint	sail
shave		wait	paint	tail
slave		trait	saint	frail
			quaint	quail
		-aim	taint	snail
		maim		trail

-ain		-ay		
gain	grain	bay	lay	say
pain	train	day	may	way
rain	chain	gay	nay	clay
brain	plain	hay	pay	play
drain	stain	jay	ray	gray

-eigh/ei-ey	-ey
eight	hey
sleigh	they
weigh	obey
weight	
neigh	
rein	
reindeer	
neighbor	

LONG E SOUNDS

-e	-ea	-each	-ead	-eak
be	pea	each	bead	beak
he	sea	beach	lead	leak
me	tea	peach	read	peak
we	flea	reach	plead	weak
she		teach		bleak
		bleach		freak
				speak

-eal	-eam	-ean	-eap	-east
deal	beam	bean	heap	east
heal	seam	lean	leap	beast
meal	team	mean	reap	feast
peal	cream	clean	cheap	least
real	dream			
seal	gleam	-eech	-eef	-eem
steal		beech	beef	deem
		leech	reef	seem

-eat	-eed	-ee	-eek	-eel
eat	deed	bee	meek	eel
beat	feed	fee	peek	feel
heat	need	see	reek	heel
meat	seed	wee	seek	peel
neat	weed	free	cheek	
seat	bleed	tree	creek	
cheat	freed	glee	sleek	
treat	greed	thee		
wheat	speed	three		

-een	-eep	-ief	-y	-ey
keen	beep	brief	carry	key
seen	deep	chief	marry	turkey
teen	jeep	grief	bunny	monkey
green	keep	thief	funny	donkey
queen	peep		sunny	
	weep	-eet		
	creep	beet	fleet	sleet
	sheep	feet	greet	sweet
		meet	sheet	

LONG I SOUNDS

-ice	-ide	-ie	-ife	-ike
lice	bide	die	life	bike
mice	hide	lie	wife	dike
nice	ride	pie	knife	hike
rice	side	tie	fife	like
vice	tide			mike
slice	wide			pike
spice	bride			spike
twice	glide			
	slide			

-ise	-ite	-ive	-igh
rise	bite	dive	high
wise	kite	five	nigh
	mite	hive	sigh
	site	live	thigh
	quite	chive	
	spite	drive	
	white		

-ile	-ime	-ine	-ipe	-ire
file	dime	dine	pipe	ire
mile	lime	fine	ripe	dire
pile	time	line	wipe	fire
tile	chime	mine	gripe	hire
vile	crime	nine	swipe	mire
smile	grime	pine		tire
while	slime	shine		wire
	prime	spine		spire

-ight	-ild	-ind	-y	-ye
fight	mild	bind	by	dye
light	wild	find	my	eye
might	child	hind	cry	lye
night		kind	dry	rye
right		mind	fry	
sight		rind	shy	
tight		wind	sky	
bright		blind	fly	
fright		grind	spy	
flight			ply	
plight			sly	

LONG O SOUND

-o	-obe	-ode	-oe	-oke
go	lobe	ode	doe	coke
no	robe	code	foe	joke
so	globe	mode	hoe	poke
ho	probe	rode	toe	choke
				smoke

-ope	-ose	-ote	-oach
cope	hose	note	coach
hope	rose	vote	poach
rope	chose	quote	roach
scope	those	wrote	
slope	close		

-ole	-ome	-one	-oad	-oal
hole	dome	bone	load	coal
mole	home	cone	road	goal
pole	Nome	lone	toad	foal
role		tone		
stole		zone		
		shone		
		stone		

-oam	-oan	-oast
foam	loan	boast
loam	moan	coast
roam	groan	roast
		toast

-olt	-ost	-ow		-oat
bolt	host	bow	flow	oat
colt	most	low	glow	boat
jolt	post	mow	slow	coat
		row	crow	goat
		sow	grow	moat
		tow	show	bloat
		blow	snow	float
				gloat

-ore	-oard	-our	-oo	-old
ore	board	four	door	old
wore	hoard	pour	moor	bold
core			floor	cold
sore				gold
tore				hold
shore				mold
score				sold
chore				told
snore				

LONG U SOUNDS

-ule	-use	-ute	-uke	-ude
mule	use	cute	duke	dude
yule	fuse	mute	Luke	rude
	muse	flute		crude

-ure	-ue	-ew	-une	-ube
pure	due	few	dune	tube
cure	sue	blew	June	cube
sure	cue	flew	tune	
	clue	slew	prune	
	true	chew		
	blue	crew		
		drew		
		grew		
		stew		

V. DIGRAPHS

Digraphs are combinations of consonants that represent one sound.

BEGINNING

ch___	sh___	wh___	th___
chin	sheep	wheel	thumb
chip	ship	white	thorn
child	show	whip	three
chicken	shoe	why	thin
chair	she	wheat	that
chain	shirt	whale	thank
cheese	sheet	whistle	thump
churn	shark	whack	throat

FINAL

___ch	___sh		___th
batch	bash		bath
catch	cash		math
match	rash		path
patch	sash		month
beach	trash		teeth
peach	rush		mouth
reach	hush		wreath
pinch			beneath
finch			

VI. THREE-LETTER CONSONANT BLENDS

str___	spr___	scr___	thr___
street	spring	scream	three
stripe	spray	screen	throw
string	sprout	scrap	thread
straw	sprig	scrape	thrill
stray	spruce	scribble	thrash
strong	spry	scrunch	throb
stroke	spread	scrabble	thrust

VII. DIPTHONGS AND -R CONTROLLED VOWELS
-OY, -OI WORDS

boy	oil	coin	noise
coy	boil	join	poise
joy	coil	joint	voice
toy	foil	point	choice
Roy	soil	moist	
troy	toil	hoist	
	broil		
	spoil		

-R CONTROLLED VOWELS

___er	___ir	___or	___ur
her	bird	word	fur
perch	third	work	burn
germ	girl	worm	turn
term	swirl	world	churn
fern	twirl	tractor	church
stern	dirt		lurch
serve	flirt		
batter	skirt		
fatter	shirt		
matter	birch		
patter			
poorer			
teacher			

CORN WORDS (-OR as in CORN)

or	cord	cork	form	born	fort
for	ford	fork	norm	corn	sort
nor	lord	pork	storm	horn	forth
		stork		morn	north
					torn
					short

CAR WORDS (-AR as in CAR)

___ar	___arm	___arn	___arp	___ark	___art	___ard
bar	farm	barn	carp	bark	art	hard
car	harm	darn	harp	dark	part	lard
far	charm	yarn	sharp	lark	cart	card
jar				hark	dart	
par				mark	hart	
scar				park	tart	
star				spark	start	
tar				shark	part	
				stark	smart	

___arch	___arge	___arsh
march	large	harsh
parch	barge	marsh
starch	charge	

BALL WORDS (-AW, -AU, and -OU as in BALL)

___all	___alk	___aw	___awl	___awn	___ought
ball	talk	saw	bawl	dawn	ought
fall	walk	law	crawl	fawn	bought
call	chalk	jaw	brawl	drawn	brought
hall	stalk	paw	shawl	yawn	fought
				lawn	

___all	___aw	___ought
mall	raw	sought
tall	draw	thought
wall	straw	cough
small	gnaw	
stall	claw	

___ause	___au	___aught
cause	auto	caught
because	haul	naught
pause	Paul	taught
clause	fault	
	vault	

-OU, -OW (-OU as in OUT, -OW as in HOW)

___ou

out	house	ounce	bound	loud
pout	louse	bounce	found	cloud
shout	mouse	pounce	hound	proud
spout	blouse	fount	mouth	pound
trout			south	round
ouch				sound
couch				ground

-OW

bow	owl	down	power
cow	cowl	gown	tower
how	fowl	town	flower
now	howl	clown	powder
vow		brown	
wow		crown	
brow		drown	
plow		frown	

-OO WORDS

1. -oo as in cook

book	rook	good	would
cook	rook	hood	should
hook	brook	wood	
look	crook	stood	
nook	shook	wool	

2. -oo as in moon

___oo	___ood	___ool	___oom	___oon
boo	food	cool	boom	boon
coo	mood	fool	doom	goon
moo	brood	pool	loom	loon
too		drool	room	moon
zoo		spool	zoom	noon

___oop	___oost	___oot	___ooth
coop	boost	boot	booth
hoop	roost	hoot	tooth
loop		loot	
droop		root	
troop		toot	
scoop		scoot	
stoop		shoot	
swoop			

VIII. OTHER PATTERNS

___sion	___tion	___ull	___ush
decision	action	bull	bush
division	motion	full	push
occasion	nation	pull	
collision	mention		
television	fraction		
mission	attention		

___ocket	___iddle	___itten	___etter
locket	fiddle	bitten	better
pocket	middle	kitten	letter
rocket	riddle	mitten	setter
socket			

Appendix F

Here is a sample of a tutor's work with a first grade child. It illustrates how a tutor can implement the strategies discussed in *Help a Child Learn to Read* within the context of a story. Every activity and mini-lesson below is based on the story of Else Minarik's *Little Bear*.

"What Will Little Bear Wear?" follows Little Bear on a snowy day. He wants to play outside, but he can't seem to get warm. He puts on a hat, a coat, and pants, but keeps coming back inside to tell his mother he's cold. Finally, he asks his mother to make him a fur coat. He takes off the hat, coat, and pants. Mother Bear explains to him that he has on his fur coat, and he goes outside, happy at last. Here Mother Bear and Little Bear are looking out the window at the snow. Little Bear decides he is cold. The discussion below is drawn from page one of the story.

Scripted Sample

WHAT WILL LITTLE BEAR WEAR?

It is cold.

See the snow.

See the snow come down.

Little Bear said, "Mother Bear,

I am cold.

See the snow.

I want something to put on."

Student _____ Grade _____ Date _____

Lesson Plan

READING: Little Bear (Minarik)

"What Will Little Bear Wear?"

•Before Reading: Previewing and Predicting

T: 1. a. Have you ever read any Little Bear books?
b. (Do you like them?)

2. Let's look at the pictures first. What do you suppose this story will be about?

Little Bear ©1957 by Else Holmeland Minarik. Used by permission of Harper Collins Publishers.

3. Would you like to read or shall I read?

•**During Reading:**

COMPREHENSION CHECK:

T: 1. What's going on? (ask at the end of each page or two)

2. a. What is Mother Bear making now?
    b. How do you know?

CRITICAL THINKING:

3. When Little Bear says he wants a fur coat, that seems funny to me. Does it seem funny to you? Why?

4. Do you like Little Bear? Why?

•**After Reading**

T: 1. Did you like that story? Tell me why.

2. What was your favorite part?

3. Do you think Mother Bear loves Little Bear? Why would you say that?

SKILLS:

1. Letter recognition, using page 1 of "What Will Little Bear Wear?"

T: Let's look at some letters. Yesterday we learned about -s. Can you find an -s on this page? There are seven. You find an -s and I'll find one. Let's find all seven.

2. Word recognition/Sound symbol correspondence

T: See this word in line 2. It's <u>See</u>. Do you hear any sounds in <u>ssee</u>? S-e-e. Now you say it. Let's make a card for <u>see</u>. You write it. *If the child cannot print <u>see</u>, make an outline of the letters and have her follow your outline.* Now let's find the word in the story. That word <u>see</u> is on this page three times. Can you find <u>see</u>? Let's read this page and every time we come to <u>see</u>, you read.

If the child cannot find <u>see</u>, redirect her. Point to the line and say, "One of those <u>sees</u> is in this line right here."

If she still does not find the word, point to each word in the line and ask, "Is that <u>see</u>? Look at the card again. Do the letters on the card match the letters in that word?"

ask, "Is that <u>see</u>? Look at the card again. Do the letters on the card match the letters in that word?"

Wait for her response and ask, "How do you know?"

You are expecting her to say, "<u>See</u> is s-e-e. That is (or that isn't) an s."

T: We know <u>see</u>. Let's learn <u>the</u> and <u>snow</u>. (Make a card for <u>the</u> and one for <u>snow</u>.)

There's a sound in <u>see</u> that's in <u>the</u> also. Do you hear <u>ee</u> in <u>see</u> and <u>the</u>? Show me the <u>e</u>. How many <u>e</u>s do you see in <u>see</u>? Good.

T: <u>See</u> starts with what letter? Look at <u>snow</u>. What letter does <u>snow</u> start with?

T: We know three words. Let's read the page and you read every time we come to 'see the snow.'

T: You said 'so.' You read, 'See the so.' Does that make sense?
What is Little Bear watching?

*Note to tutor: Just from page 1 of *Little Bear*, you could also work on the following skills:

a. word patterns with

   -am (ham, jam, ram, Sam, etc.)

   -it (bit, fit, hit, kit, mit, pit, sit)

   -not (dot, got, lot, hot)

   -hat (bat, cat, fat, mat, pat, rat, sat) etc., etc.

b. letter identification (for any letter)

c. capitalization

Show the child that names, I, and the first letter of the first word of each sentence all begin with upper case letters. Ask her to point to all the upper case letters on the page.

d. end punctuation

e. sound-symbol identification

Make sure the word is easily decoded phonetically until the child is ready for more difficult phonics.

f. context clues

WRITING

T: What would you like to write? We can write about you or we can write about Little Bear.

S: About Little Bear

T: What shall we say about Little Bear?

S: 'Little Bear is my friend. He already has his coat on.'

T: *(Repeat what the child says.)* 'Little Bear is my friend. He already has his coat on.' Okay. Shall I write or would you like to?

S: You write.

T: I'll write but you can write too. Which words do you want to write?

S: Little Bear

T: Let's write on cards. *(Adjust the size of the card to accomodate the child's fine motor skills; let him write on 3x5", 5x7", 81/2 x 11", or the sidewalk if need be.)*

   <u>Little</u>. Do you hear any of the letters in *Little*?

   <u>Little</u>.

S: Un-un

T: Well, you spell <u>little</u> L-i-t-t-l-e. Now you write it. L-i-t-t-l-e. We use the upper case L because Little Bear is a name just as Maria is your name. Good. Now <u>Bear</u>. Do you hear any letters in <u>Bear</u>? <u>Bear</u>.

S: Yep, <u>BBB</u>

T: Good, write down a B, now e-a-r. Good. I'll write the rest. *(Tutor writes)* Now let's **<u>read</u>** it. *(Tutor reads* "Little Bear is my friend. He already has his coat on" *two or three times.)* Now you read it. *(Student reads two or three times.)* Good!

T: Now show me which word is <u>Little</u>. How do you know? Which word is _____? *(pick out five to seven words).*

T: Let's mix up these words and make some of our own sentences.

(*Note: You may make word cards with all or some of these words. The child can then make his or her own sentences.)

T: Let's read our new sentences:

My friend is Little Bear.

Little Bear has his coat.

My friend has his coat.

(Notice that the writing portion also includes reading, speaking, and skill practice.)

Reading for pleasure: *For the last few minutes, read something different just for pleasure. Say to the child,*

T: I was looking for something special to read to you and I found this comic strip. Do you like "Peanuts"?

After reading, say,

T: Next time, if you wish, you may bring something to read to me or something that you want me to read to you.

59 Different Words from "What Will Little Bear Wear" - approximately 75% are Dolch

a: a, and, am, again

b: bear, be

c: cold, cannot, come, can, coat

d: down, do

f: for, fur

h: have, hat, here, hurray, head, he

i: I, it, is, in

l: little

m: mother, made, my

n: now, not

o: on, of, oh, out

p: put, play, pants

s: see, something, snow, said, so, she

t: the, took, to, there, too, think, that

w: what, was, will, went, wear, want

y: your, you, yes

Appendix G

Student_____ Grade _____ Date _____

Lesson Plan

Reading:

Comprehension Check:

Skills:

Writing:

Reading for pleasure:

Bibliography

Works Cited

Applebee, A., & Langer, J. (1983). Instructional scaffolding: Reading and writing as natural language activities. *Language Arts, 60,* 168-75.

Asher, J. (1982). *Learning another language through actions: The complete teacher's guidebook.* Los Gatos, CA: Sky Oaks.

Asher, J. (1983). The total physical response. Presentation at the California Education Association, San Francisco, January 14.

Bloom, B. (1984). The search for methods of group instruction as effective as one-to-one tutoring. *Educational Leadership, 41* (8), 4-17.

Bruner, J.S. (1964). The course of cognitive growth. *American Psychologist, 19,* 1-15.

Bruner, J.S. (1978). *The child's conception of language.* New York: Springer-Verlag.

Bruner, J.S. (1986). *Actual minds, possible worlds.* Cambridge: Harvard University Press.

Bruner, J.S., & Olson, R. (1980). Symbols and texts as tools of thought. *Interchange, 8*(4), 1-15.

Clay, M.M., & Cazden, C.B. (1990). A Vygotskian interpretation of reading recovery. In L. Moll (Ed.), *Vygotsky and Education.* New York: Cambridge University Press.

Cohen, P., Kulik, J.A., & Kulik, C. (1982). Educational outcomes of tutoring: A meta-analysis of findings. *American Educational Research Journal, 19,* 237-248.

Day, Alexandra. (1985). *Good dog, Carl.* Hong Kong: Green Tiger Press.

Devin-Sheehan, L., Feldman, R.S., & Allen, V.L. (1976). Research on children tutoring children: A critical review. *Review of Education Research, 46,* 355-385.

Dr. Seuss. (1960). *Green eggs and ham.* New York: Beginner Books by Random House.

Elkind, D. (1988). *Miseducation: Preschoolers at risk.* New York: Knopf.

Elkind, D. (1989). *The hurried child: Growing up too fast too soon.* New York: Addison-Wesley.

Field, Eugene. "Wynken, Blynken, and Nod." In Edna Johnson, Evelyn Sickels, & F.C. Sayers (Eds.), *Anthology of Children's Literature.* Boston: Houghton Mifflin, 1959.

Fromkin, V. & Rodman, R. (1997). *An introduction to language.* 6th ed. Orlando: Harcourt Brace.

Gaffney, J.S., & Anderson, R.C. (1991). Two-tiered scaffolding: Congruent processes of teaching and learning. In E.H. Hiebert (Ed.) *Literacy for a diverse society* (pp. 184-198). New York: Teachers College Press.

Greenwood, C.R., Delquardi, J.C., & Hall, R.V. (1989). Longitudinal effects of classwide peer tutoring. *Journal of Educational Psychology, 81,* 371-383.

Hiebert, E.H. (1994a). Reading Recovery in the United States: What difference does it make to an age cohort? *Educational Researcher, 23,* 15-25.

Hiebert, E.H. (1994b). A small-group literacy intervention with Chapter I students. In E.H. Hiebert & B.M. Taylor (Eds.), *Getting reading right from the start* (pp. 85-106). Needham Heights, MA: Allyn & Bacon.

Hoyt, F. (1906). The place of grammar in the elementary curriculum. *Teachers College Record, 7,* 483-84.

Irving, Washington. *Rip Van Winkle and The Legend of Sleepy Hollow.* New York: MacMillan, 1951.

Jenkins, J.R., & Jenkins, L.M. (1987, March). Making peer tutoring work. *Educational Leadership,* 64-68.

Juel, C. (1988). Learning to read and write: A longitudinal study of fifty-four children from first through fourth grade. *Journal of Educational Psychology, 80,* 437-447.

Juel, C. (1991). Cross-age tutoring between student athletes and at-risk children. *The Reading Teacher, 45,* 178-186.

Juel, C. (1994). *Learning to read and write in one elementary school.* New York: Springer-Verlag.

Juel, C. (1996). What makes tutoring effective? *Reading Research Quarterly, 31,* 268-286.

Juel, C., Griffith, P.L., & Gough, P.B. (1986). Acquisition of literacy: A longitudinal study of children in first and second grade. *Journal of Educational Psychology, 78,* 243-255.

Longfellow, Henry Wadsworth. "Hiawatha's Childhood" (from *The Song of Hiawatha*). In Edna Johnson, Evelyn Sickels, & F.C. Sayers, (Eds.), *Anthology of Children's Literature.* Boston: Houghton Mifflin, 1959.

Lowell, J.R. (1871). *The vision of Sir Launfal.* Boston: Osgood and Co.

McLeary, E. (1971). Reports of results of Tutorial Reading Project. *The Reading Teacher, 24,* 556-559.

Minarik, E.H. (1957). *Little bear.* New York: Harper and Row.

Piaget, J. (1954). *The construction of reality in the child.* New York: Basic Books.

Richard-Amato, P.A. (1996). *Making it happen: Interaction in the second language classroom.* 2nd ed. White Plains, NY: Longman.

Riley, J.W. (1916). *Complete Works.* 10 vols. New York: Bobbs-Merrill.

Sendak, M. (1988). *Where the wild things are.* New York: Harper Trophy.

Topping, K., & Whitely, M. (1990). Participant evaluation of parent-tutored and peer-tutored projects in reading (Yorkshire). *Educational Research, 32,* 14-32.

Topping, K. (1987). Peer tutored paired reading: Outcome data from ten projects. *Educational Psychology, 7* (2), 133-145.

Wasik, B. & Slavin, R. (1993). Preventing early reading failure with one-to-one tutoring: A review of five programs. *Reading Research Quarterly, 28* (2), 179-194

Wertsch, J.V. et al. (1980). The adult-child dyad as a problem solving system. *Child Development, 51,* 1215-1221.

Wertsch, J.V. (1984). The zone of proximal development: Some conceptual issues. In B. Rogoff & J.V. Wertsch (Eds.), *Children's learning in the zone of proximal development* (pp. 7-18). San Francisco: Jossey-Bass.

Whittier, J.G. The barefoot boy. In *American poetry: The nineteenth century.* (1996). New York: The Library of America.

Williams, J.M. (1975). *Origins of the English language: A social and linguistic history.* New York: MacMillan.

Wood, D., Bruner, J.S., & Ross, G. (1976). The role of tutoring in problem solving. *Journal of Child Psychology & Psychiatry, 17,* 89-100.

Bibliography for Further Reading

Adams, M. J. (1990). *Beginning to read: Thinking and learning about print.* Cambridge: The MIT Press.

Adams, M. J. (1995, Summer). Resolving the great debate. *American Educator, 19* (2), 7 - 20.

Baker, S. K., Simmons, D. C., & Kameenui, E. J. (1995). *Vocabulary acquisition: Synthesis of the research* (Technical Report No. 13). Eugene: National Center to Improve the Tools of Educators, University of Oregon.

Baker, S. K., Simmons, D. C., & Kameenui, E. J. (1995). *Vocabulary Acquisition: Curricular and instructional implications for diverse learners* (Technical Report No. 14). Eugene: National Center to Improve the Tools of Educators, University of Oregon.

Baker, S. K., Simmons, D. C., & Kameenui, E. J. (1995). *Characteristics of students with diverse learning and curricular needs.* Eugene: National Center to Improve the Tools of Educators, University of Oregon.

Beck, I. & Juel, C. (1995). The role of decoding in learning to read. *American Educator, 19* (2), 8-25.

Blachman, B. (1991). *Getting ready to read: Learning how print maps to speech.* Bethesda, MD: U.S. Department of Health and Human Services, National Institute of Child Health and Human Development.

Brufee, K. (1973). Collaborative learning: Some practical models. *College English, 34,* 579-586.

Brufee, K. (1984). Collaborative writing and the "conversation of mankind." *College English, 46,* 635-652.

Brufee, K. (1986). Social construction, language, and the authority of knowledge: A bibliographical essay. *College English, 48* (8), 773-788.

Colvin, R.J. (1997). *I speak English: A guide to teaching English to speakers of other languages - listening, speaking, reading, writing.* Syracuse: Literacy Volunteers of America.

Cassidy, F.G., and Ringler, R.N., eds. (1971). *Bright's Old English grammar and reader.* 3rd ed., 2nd printing. New York: Holt, Rinehart, and Winston.

Chard, D. J., Simmons, D. C., & Kameenui, E. J. (1995). *Word recognition: Curricular and instructional implications for diverse learners* (Technical Report No. 16). Eugene: National Center to Improve the Tools of Educators, University of Oregon.

Chard, D. J., Simmons, D. C., & Kameenui, E. J. (1995b). *Understanding the primary role of word recognition in the reading process: Synthesis of research on beginning reading* (Technical Report No. 15). Eugene: National Center to Improve the Tools of Educators, University of Oregon.

Cheatham, J.B., Colvin, R.J., and Laminack, L.L. (1993). *TUTOR: A collaborative approach to literacy instruction.* Syracuse: Literacy Volunteers of America.

Clay, M.M. (1979). *Reading: The patterning of complex behavior.* Portsmouth, N.H.: Heinemann.

Clay, M.M. (1985). *The early detection of reading difficulties.* Exeter, N.H.: Heinemann.

DeBoer, J. (1959). Grammar in language teaching. *Elementary English, 36,* 412-21.

Dickson, S. V., Simmons, D. C., & Kameenui, E. J. (1995). *Text organization: Curricular and instructional implications for diverse learners* (Technical Report No. 19). Eugene: National Center to Improve the Tools of Educators, University of Oregon.

Dickson, S. V., Simmons, D. C., & Kameenui, E. J. (1995). *Text organization and its relation to reading comprehension: A synthesis of the research* (Technical Report No. 17). Eugene: National Center to Improve the Tools of Educators, University of Oregon.

Fish, S. (1980). *Is there a text in this class? The authority of interpretative communities.* Cambridge: Harvard University Press.

Glass, G., Cahen, L., Smith, M.L. & Filby, N. (1982). *School class size.* Beverly Hills: Sage.

Goodlad, J. (1984). *A place called school: Prospects for the future.* New York: McGraw-Hill.

Goodman, K.S. (1986). *What's whole in whole language?* Portsmouth, N.H.: Heinemann.

Goodman, Y. (1978). Kid watching: An alternative to testing. *Journal of National Elementary Principals, 57,* 41-45.

Graves, D. (1980). Research update: A new look at writing research. *Language Arts, 57,* 913-919.

Gunn, B. K., Simmons, D. C., & Kameenui, E. J. (1995). *Emergent literacy: Synthesis of the research* (Technical Report No. 19). Eugene: National Center to Improve the Tools of Educators, University of Oregon.

Gunn, B. K., Simmons, D. C., & Kameenui, E. J. (1995). *Emergent literacy: Curricular and instructional implications for diverse learners* (Technical Report No. 20). Eugene: National Center to Improve the Tools of Educators, University of Oregon.

Hiebert, E.H. (1994). Becoming literate through authentic tasks: Evidence and adaptations. In R.B. Ruddell, M.R. Ruddell, & H. Singer (Eds.), *Theoretical models and processes of reading* (4th ed., pp. 391-413). Newark, DE: International Reading Association.

Kameenui, E. J., Simmons, D. C., Baker, S., Chard, D., Dickson, S., Gunn, B., Smith, S., Sprick, M., & Lin, S. (1995). *Effective strategies for teaching beginning reading.* Eugene: National Center to Improve the Tools of Educators, University of Oregon.

Liberman, I. Y., Shankweiler, D., & Liberman, A. M. (1989). *The alphabet principle and learning to read.* Bethesda, MD: U.S. Department of Health and Human Services, National Institute of Child Health and Human Development.

Lyon, G. R. (Ed.) (1994). *Frames of reference for the assessment of learning disabilities.* Baltimore: Paul H. Brookes.

Lyon, G. R. (1995). Toward a definition of dyslexia. *Annals of Dyslexia, 45,* 3-27.

Lyon, G. R., Gray, D. B., Kavanagh, J. F., & Krasnegot, N. A. (Eds.). (1993). *Better understanding learning disabilities.* Baltimore: Paul H. Brookes.

Lyon, G. R. & Krasnegot, N. A. (Eds.). (1995). *Attention, memory, and executive function.* Baltimore: Paul H. Brookes.

Moats, L. C. (1994). The missing foundation in teacher education: Knowledge of the structure of spoken and written language. *Annals of Dyslexia, 44,* 81-102.

Moats, L. C. (1995). The missing foundation in teacher education. *American Educator, 19* (2), 9-19.

Moats, L. C. & Lyon, G.R. (1995). Wanted: Teachers with knowledge of language. *Topics in Language Disorders, 15,* 10-21.

Moffett, J. (1968). *Teaching the universe of discourse.* Boston: Houghton Mifflin.

Moffett, J. (1976). *Student-centered language arts and reading.* Boston: Houghton Mifflin.

Nagy, P., & Griffiths, A. (1982). Limitations of recent research relating Piaget's theory of adolescent thought. *Review of Educational Research, 52,* 513-556.

Piaget, J. (1952). *The origins of intelligence in children* (M. Cook, Trans.). New York: International University Press.

Piaget, J. (1970, May). Conversations. *Psychology Today,* pp. 25-32.

Piaget, J. (1971). *The science of education and the psychology of the child.* New York: Viking Press.

Piaget, J. (1972). Intellectual evolution from adolescence to adulthood. *Human Development, 15,* 1-12.

Robarge, J., & Flexer, B. (1979). Further examinations of formal operational reasoning abilities. *Child Development, 50,* 478-484.

Rosenblatt, L. (1978). *The reader, the text, the poem.* Carbondale: Southern Illinois University Press.

Slavin, R.E., Madden, N.A., Karweit, N.L., Dolan, L., and Wasik, B.A. (1992). *Success for all: A relentless approach to prevention and early intervention in elementary schools.* Arlington, VA: Educational Research Service.

Smith, F. (1973). *Psycholinguistics and reading.* New York: Holt, Rinehart, & Winston.

Smith, S. B., Simmons, D. C., & Kameenui, E. J. (1995). *Synthesis of research on phonological awareness: Principles and implications for reading acquisition* (Technical Report No. 21). Eugene: National Center to Improve the Tools of Educators, University of Oregon.

Smith, S. B., Simmons, D. C., & Kameenui, E. J. (1995b). *Phonological awareness: Curricular and instructional implications for diverse learners* (Technical Report No. 22). Eugene: National Center to Improve the Tools of Educators, University of Oregon.

Stahl, S. A., Osborn, J., & Lehr, F. (1990). *Beginning to read: Thinking and learning about print, A summary.* Champaign: The University of Illinois.

Teale, William. (1991). An interview with Marilyn Adams. *Language Arts, 68,* 206-212.

Vygotsky, L. (1962). *Thought and language.* (E. Hanfmann & G. Vakar, Trans.). Cambridge: M.I.T.

Wasik, B.A. & Slavin, R.E. (1990). *Preventing early reading failure with one-to-one tutoring: A best-evidence synthesis.* Paper presented at the annual convention of the American Educational Research Association, Boston.